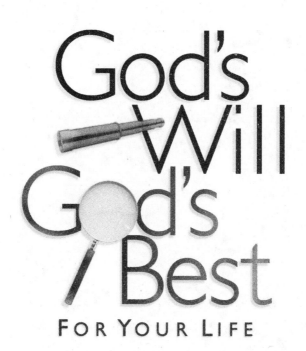

God's Will God's Best

FOR YOUR LIFE

JOSH McDOWELL
KEVIN JOHNSON

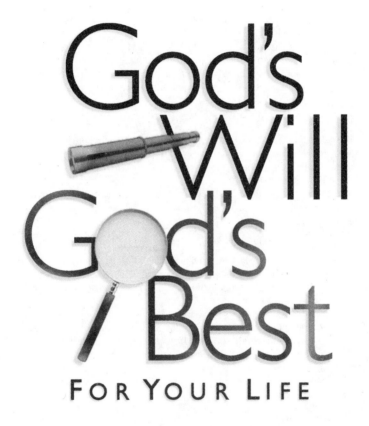

God's Will God's Best

FOR YOUR LIFE

BETHANYHOUSE
MINNEAPOLIS, MINNESOTA

Published by Bethany House Publishers
11400 Hampshire Avenue South
Bloomington, Minnesota 55438
www.bethanyhouse.com

Bethany House Publishers is a division of
Baker Publishing Group, Grand Rapids, Michigan

Printed in the United States of America

Library of Congress Cataloging-in-Publication Data
McDowell, Josh.
   God's will, God's best / by Josh McDowell and Kevin Johnson.
      p. cm.
   Includes bibliographical references.
   ISBN 0-7642-2328-3 (pbk.)
      1. Teenagers—Religious life. 2. God—Will. I. Johnson, Kevin (Kevin
   Walter) II. Title.
   BV4531.2 .M223 2000
   248.8'3—dc21   00-9924

Cover by Bill Chiaravalle

17 18 19 20 21 22 23   12 11 10 9 8 7 6

To our wives,

Dottie and Lyn

for being our lifelong partners in seeking God's best

JOSH McDOWELL, internationally known speaker, author, and traveling representative of Campus Crusade for Christ, International, has authored or coauthored more than fifty books, including *The Disconnected Generation* and *Don't Check Your Brains at the Door*. Josh and his wife, Dottie, have four children and live in Dallas, Texas.

KEVIN JOHNSON is the creator of the first-of-its-kind *Pray the Scriptures Bible* and the bestselling author or coauthor of more than fifty books and study Bibles for adults, students, and children. His training includes an MDiv from Fuller Theological Seminary and a BA in English and print journalism from the University of Wisconsin–River Falls. With a background as a youth worker, senior nonfiction book editor, and teaching pastor, he now leads Emmaus Road Church in metro Minneapolis. Kevin is married to Lyn, and they have three grown children.

Learn more at kevinjohnsonbooks.com.

Contents

CHAPTER 1

Getting Into God's Plan for You

Imagine that every afternoon as you walk home from school you pass an ice cream cart. Each day the ice cream vendor motions to you from across the street to hand you an ice cream cone—cone after cone in what adds up to an endless assortment, an explosion of flavor each day. Time after time you savor a new taste like nothing you have experienced before. You walk away satisfied and happy, with a grin so big you could lodge an ice cream cone sideways in your mouth. Every cone fills you up until your next helping.

Life Should Be So Good

Okay. Stop imagining. Think instead about your everyday life—and about the future you would like to live. Now go back to the start of this page and—in place of the words *ice cream*—substitute whatever you think would make your life incredibly happy.

Think big. Think real. Forget about make-believe

wishing stars or wasted birthday wishes, and ask your-self this deep question: If life could hand you what you really want, what would it be?

In a survey pollster George Barna conducted for my *Right From Wrong* campaign, almost four thousand churchgoing youth produced this list of the top seven things they want out of life:

* *Life lived to the extreme.* Not the bungee-jump-ing kind of extreme, but having health, free-dom, and the physical strength to live life to the max.

* *True love for life.* That's not surprising. In years of meeting people all over the world, I have found that every human alive has one of two fears: that you won't be loved, or that you won't be able to love.

* *Close personal friendships.* Who wants to go through life alone?

* *Meaningful work.* After spending a dozen years at school in assigned seats, you maybe dream of actually picking your work—and having it mean more than a paycheck.

* *Enjoyment of the comforts of life.* That's a nat-

ural desire. Misery may love company, but no one loves misery.

✳ *A close relationship with God.* Not highest on the list but important to many and, I believe, the key to all the rest.

✳ *The chance to make a difference in the world.* Most people want significance. They want their lives to matter, to leave their mark, to do good in other people's lives. You probably do too.

The Best Things in Life

If you had those seven things, you'd be living happy. In fact, if you knew to name all seven things as your top desires in life, you would be a winner. That's a great list of life's most important things.

Wouldn't it be great to actually have those wants fulfilled?

If I told you there was a way to guarantee you those things, you might think I was fooling.

But what if I was telling the truth? What if I told you there was a foolproof plan for you to live life to the extreme, love and be loved, make friends, know God, have meaningful work, enjoy life, and make the world a better place? Yet what if I didn't make that promise to you, but God did?

Suppose God had a plan that could give you those hot desires of your heart. He could, you know. He knows your present and can alter your future. I am guessing that you would want in on God's plan. I would.

The Tunnel of Life

Think back to that ice cream cart. This time imagine it on the sidewalk of a big city—in Manhattan, to be exact, home to all of the skyscrapers in New York City. Put it right next to a hot dog vendor and a newsstand and a staircase down to the subway. Got the picture? Except now you're in a car, a mile from the entrance to the Holland Tunnel, the one route out of the city that will take you where you need to go. You inch your car forward, jostling with other cars and cabs and playing chicken with buses.

You could sit for hours waiting for traffic to unplug. But what if there were a better way to do things? What if someone above the maze of buildings could direct your car down the right streets and alleys to make your exit? And what if you could blast through the tunnel at two hundred miles an hour, driving on the ceiling like in some cool science fiction movie?

Your future is like that tunnel. It looms somewhere in front of you. You *must* enter. You want to get there in good time. And you would probably want some help to make it through without nicks, dents, or crashes.

Welcome to Jason's World

Jason has just started his senior year of high school. From the time he was eight he was sure he wanted to go to college and study biology—until he actually took biology, that is, and found he had to do dissections with one hand on the knife and the other holding his nose.

On top of that discouraging experience, Jason keeps hearing about poor job prospects for biologists and high educational requirements to succeed in the field. When his older sister gets a high-paying computer job straight out of technical school, Jason thinks about by-passing four-year college altogether. But now he has applied to a popular out-of-state public university, despite his parents' strong desire for him to go to a small Christian school an hour away. Add to Jason's chaos some deep fondness for a girl he met at school—only a junior, so if he goes away to college he feels he will never see her again.

Welcome to Jason's world of turmoil.

It's your world too.

Jason struggles with all kinds of questions—if and where to attend college, what career suits him best, what relationships to carry into the future, and questions about how church and faith will fit into his life once he leaves home. He is trying to find life, love, and happiness. It sounds like he's going to need help if he ever hopes to meet even one or two of those top seven desires.

Like Jason, you're trying to figure out your life too. Well, God is tracking you from above the maze—He sees your past, present, and future and can tell you exactly how to go. Better than any Global Positioning System, He comprehends all the facts and feelings and interactions of your life. Now, wouldn't it be great if God would let you in on His view of things? If you knew what God knew . . . if God was willing to share His route for your life . . . then you would know how to navigate life and fulfill all your desires.

Like I said, I think you would want in on God's plan.

The Burning Question

As I have spoken to Christian youth around the world for the past thirty years, I have heard one question asked a thousand different ways: "What is God's plan for my life?" The question comes out in different words: "What college should I go to?" "Does God want me to get married?" "Who is the right person to marry?" "What about this major—or that job?" "What is the real purpose of my life?" But whatever the words, the plea is always the same: Can you tell me what path God wants me to take?

Seeking God's best is critical for people of all ages, but especially for you as a young person. In the next ten years you will lay the foundation for your adult life, dealing with three of the biggest issues you will ever face:

✻ *who will guide you*—whether or not you will allow God to lead you. You are finding your *master*.

✻ *who, and if, you will marry*—a doubly difficult decision because it requires someone else's agreement. You are finding, and deciding whether or not to have, a *mate*.

✻ *what you will do with your life*—your career and the steps to take to get there. You are discovering your *mission*.

Can You Believe God Wants What's Good?

So if you are looking for the way to fulfill your deepest desires, where do you find help?

I won't make you wait any longer for the secret. Every one of the top seven desires those students named—the same desires you probably have for your own life—reflects a God-given need. And here's that guarantee again: God has plans to meet those needs. Plans He has promised to deliver on. Read this:

> "For I know the plans I have for you," declares the Lord, "plans to prosper you and not to harm you, plans to give you hope and a future." (Jeremiah 29:11)

Read the same thing from another spot in the Bible:

And my God will meet all your needs according to his glorious riches in Christ Jesus. (Philippians 4:19)

And in case you're doubting His promise, God says it a third time:

Delight yourself in the Lord and he will give you the desires of your heart. (Psalm 37:4)

Read those verses again. Each shows a God beyond your wildest hopes—a God whose plan is the best for your life. He wants you to live life to the extreme, love and be loved, make friends, know Him, have meaningful work, enjoy life, and make the world a better place.

Making Good on the Guarantee

Does that sound too good to be true? If anyone but God were making that promise, you would have every reason to call it *hype, spin,* or worse.

And if I said those words on my own, you would be absolutely right. But I didn't.

God wants your best interests served.

God wants you happy in His ways.

God has a plan to give you your desires.

God has the power to provide anything.

So how does that happen?

If you want to find out how you become part of God's plan to grant you the longings of your heart, go back and read the first part of the verse—the first part of Psalm 37:4, that is.

"*Delight yourself in the Lord* and he will give you the desires of your heart" (italics added).

You knew there had to be a catch. But it's not a catch. It's a condition. *If* you delight yourself in the Lord, *then* He will give you the desires of your heart. And it's a condition you will want to fulfill.

How to Be Happy in God

So God fulfills your heart's desire when you "delight yourself" in Him.

What's that mean?

You probably never in your life have claimed you "delight" in something. "Delight" is a word you last heard uttered by your first-grade teacher, as in "Class, we are delighted to have Firefighter Smith with us today to explain how to avoid third-degree burns."

Hearing Psalm 37:4 worded differently might help you catch the true meaning of *delight*: "*Be happy with the Lord*" says God's Word Translation. "*Enjoy serving the Lord*" reads the New Century Version. Delighting in God isn't mere warm-fuzziness. It's not a busing-trays-with-a-bad-attitude kind of serving. It's living happy, knowing that you can belong to and dedicate your life to the flawless God of the universe, choosing to allow Him to lead you to the good places *He* chooses.

"My sophomore year I really wanted the lead role in

the school play," Sarah admits. "I didn't even make the cast. I was so ashamed to tell my mom, that I didn't say a thing until a neighbor told her. After I thought about it for a while, though, I decided I was being a brat and that this was my chance to do things God's way. It was more important to be a servant than to have everyone see me, so I signed up for stage crew. I finally noticed some of the people helping backstage. We're still friends."

Delighting yourself in God and His plans is God's way of giving you the real desires of your heart—a life He designed for you to enjoy.

You also need to know the opposite fact: Outside of God's plan, you won't fulfill your deep longings.

The God Who Meets Your Needs

Suppose you were a car. Not a stripped-down rental, but the world's best. Not a production model, but a one-of-a-kind vehicle built by an automotive genius.

If you were that car, who alone would completely understand you? Who could craft your parts? Who would describe every mechanism in how you run? And who would be there to fix that one-of-a-kind car if you broke down or crashed?

Only your creator could know you like that.

You are more unique than any car could ever be. You also have a mind of your own. You can drive away from God by picking your own way. Yet I believe God alone can meet your deepest desires. Why?

* Those good things you want are *needs He built in you*. As a unique creation you need unique care. God alone knows exactly what you need to make you hum.

* Those good things you want are *His alone to give*. Belonging, love, purpose, significance— God invented those.

* Those good things you want *only work when you pursue them His way*.

Take love and sex, a topic we will check out in chapter 3. God created love. But love and sex done outside the boundaries God created will explode on you. So will anything else in life that is done outside God's plan.

The truth is those good things you want are only available when you stick close to God. Just like you wouldn't drive a one-of-a-kind car too far from its designer, you can't expect to experience God's care when you joyride far from your caregiver.

This Toy Not for Children Under Three

God is ready to give to you, but He is only ready to give you His best things.

When you were little you probably went to discount

stores and saw all sorts of action figures in the toy aisles. I'm not talking about the ever popular Barbies or now-extinct Power Rangers. I mean the three-year-old shoppers with angry foot-stompin' action.

Hear the promise again: If you delight yourself in God, He will give you the desires of your heart. But hear this problem: You and I are not 100 percent perfect in delighting in God—wanting His ways, valuing what He thinks is important, making our desires conform to His desires. Some days we are like three-year-olds who want more toys than we could ever play with, toys that don't fit our age, or even toys that could hurt us. And oh, do we stomp.

We aren't toddlers. But God still knows better than to cater to our every whim. God wants so much to give us what is good that He won't give us what is bad. He meets our good needs, not our gimmie-gimmies.

Melissa is legally of age to drink alcohol and be in bars. She has some huge choices to make about how to treat her body and where to hang out. The last time her look-alike underage sister came to visit her at college, she panicked. "Pray that I can find my fake ID so Jessie can come with us!" she pleaded to a friend.

That isn't how God works! "God, help me find my fake ID so my sister can sneak into a bar and get plastered" isn't a desire God wants to answer. He isn't going to help you down a path that will take you into deep trouble.

A Different Kind of Fun

If you are serious about grabbing hold of your heart's deepest desires, then living close to the God who knows you, loves you, and desires to fill your heart with untamed happiness hardly sounds like a catch. And knowing that God won't deliver on your unwise desires isn't a catch either—unless you consider things like guardrails on cliff-edged mountain roads a bad idea.

God isn't necessarily doling out the kind of success people dream about from Hollywood to Nashville to Manhattan, the kind that over-the-top cheerleaders, jocks, and brains might cherish. God has been around for a while and He has an eternally wise perspective: The best things of life aren't big houses, fast cars, the best job, highest pay, or whopper authority. You can have a low IQ and feel a sense of purpose—if you know that God values you. You can have far less money than you would like and still find rest—if you allow God to supply your needs. You can be paralyzed from the neck down and live life to the extreme—if you are committed to finding God's best for you.

Patrick was twenty when he slid into second base in a casual softball game. He never got up. His spinal cord was injured and his body was paralyzed from the shoulders down. His paralysis, however, didn't stop him from finishing college and making a life with his wife and children. "You don't know what life will bring," Patrick says. "But if God is at the center of your life, everything else falls into place."

Will you always get exactly what you expect? No. Will you always have it tough? No. God won't grant your wild, out-of-His-will wishes. But He is into fulfilling your deepest desires. Waiting and trusting will bring reward, satisfaction, a surprise around every corner. It's God's kind of fun, and it's the best fun there is.

Desire God First

The Bible says that "every good and perfect gift is from above, coming down from the Father of the heavenly lights, who does not change like shifting shadows" (James 1:17). *Every* good gift comes from *God*.

You and thousands of other students came up with a pretty good list of the best gifts in life. If you were God, who would you *not* want to drop all kinds of good stuff on? I'll be honest. He doesn't look out for your classmates who already look out for number one. He doesn't lend a hand to men and women who step on colleagues to climb the corporate ladder. And He isn't interested in handing you His out-of-this-world ice cream cones if you go through life selfishly grabbing everything for yourself.

God is happy, though, to show His goodness to people who want nothing more than to know and follow Him: "For the eyes of the Lord range throughout the earth," says 2 Chronicles 16:9, "to strengthen those whose hearts are fully committed to him." If you delight yourself in Him, He will give you the desires of your heart. He is going to lead you into His best for your life.

It's like God is saying, "Step through that door of desiring *me* first, and I guarantee you will find what you're looking for—and much more."

I Want to Live Life
to the Extreme

My parents know they can't control me," Brittany grins. "But that look they give me really bugs me. The worst is when Dad says he wonders where his little girl has gone—the one who trusted him and looked up to him. That's when I scream, 'I'm not a little girl!' But part of me knows he's right. Some days I can almost believe that Mom and Dad only want what's best for me. But I want to make up my own mind about stuff. I won't—I can't—go back. But I'm not sure how to go forward."

There's Something Fishy Going on Around Here

If you are thinking any of those things about your own life, you are normal. You are even mostly right. You aren't a little girl or boy. Your parents won't run your life forever. You can't go back to the way it was when you were a tiny tyke. But you are also in a crunch to figure out a positive way to go forward in life.

Being your age is a rush to fill the desires of your heart. You might think that what you lack is freedom—and that an escape from your parents' ways is your key to wild happiness. Right now Brittany hates it when anyone lays rules on her, but she especially resents her parents' expectations. She wants control over what she does, when she does it, and who she does it with.

To some people, that is what it means to find happiness. But I think there is a better way to find the radically good life we long for.

Even Brittany suspects that.

Think about this: As long as a fish is where he is designed to be—swimming in water—he flourishes. But a fish that wants to dance the mamba on the floor will be one unhappy fish.

I have proof of this, because there's this girl who keeps a large tank of fish. She has several large barbs—beautiful fish as shiny as tinfoil and almost as big as your hand. One day a fish went strolling outside the tank. Do you know how far that fish got? About ten feet. Not bad for a fish out of water but I bet the fish wished the fun had lasted longer.

Real freedom is knowing your God-given potential and using it. It comes from understanding what God designed for you to accomplish and then doing it. A fish can think "I've got to be free. Let me go live in the atmosphere" all he wants. But he still can't breathe air. And he's not wise to try.

Those Desires of Your Heart

What we're going to see is that unless you want to spend your last gasps flipping around on the floor, your happiness depends on finding a way to fulfill the desires of your heart that is *wise*. It's how you get into God's best.

The purpose of *God's Will, God's Best* is to show you how you can find God's plan for every area of your life. We want you to know how you can unlock your heart's desires. But before we talk about how to go there, let's remind ourselves where we are wanting to get. What kind of happy life are you really aiming at? Let's look at that list we saw a few pages back and name those needs:

* You want to love and be loved. That's a normal human desire *to feel loved*.

* You want to be surrounded by good friends. That's a need for *belonging*.

* You want to be close to God. That's called *intimacy with God*.

* You want a meaningful career. That's a cry for *purpose*.

* You want to enjoy the good things of life. That's your need for *rest*.

❋ You want your life to matter. That's looking for *significance*.

And the topic for this chapter:

❋ You want to live life to the extreme. That's the sum of many needs: *competence* and *uniqueness* balanced with *self-control* and *safety*.

In a way, this desire rolls together all your other desires. It's a vital *attitude*. It's bold *actions*. It's valuable *assets* you need to do life well.

Extreme Desire

But here's the big question: How badly do you want that *real* good stuff of life?

Are you willing to do what it takes to live life to the extreme?

In the X Games—the Olympics of extreme sports—men and women compete in everything from winter mountain biking to "Big Air" snowboarding to street luge. (That last one is seventy miles an hour, half an inch off the ground, with no brakes!) But the most extreme sport is skyboarding—parachuting with a snowboard . . . minus the parachute for the first few thousand feet. To train as a skyboarder costs tens of thousands of dollars a year. A top pro team makes an average of five hundred jumps in a year. Those jumps last only a minute each. You can do the math: In an entire year, pro skyboarders get only eight hours of actual in-the-air time.

Are skyboarders insane? Maybe.

Skilled? Definitely.

Dedicated? Absolutely.

Skyboarders have two secrets for getting the gusto they want. Secret #1: They have an *extreme* desire for an *extreme* experience. Secret #2: They learn wise ways to live out their extreme desire.

There are some limits to their lunacy. Skyboarders all jump with parachutes. They all employ dependable planes and skilled pilots. They all put safety before style because they know that untrained muscles and wrong moves snap limbs.

See, the ultimate extreme athletes know that breaking the rules means breaking bones—or worse.

Real life is the same way. You find God's best when you find God's wise way of doing life.

Cool, Mean, and Fast

Life breaks when you try to meet normal, good needs in unwise ways.

Two girls walk into an elevator. "I know what it takes to get to the top in this world," one says to her friend. "You gotta be cool, you gotta be mean, you gotta be fast. That's me—cool, mean, and fast. I got it."

Those girls probably want no more or less than

what you want from life. But being cool, mean, and fast won't take them to the top any more than a broken elevator gets you where you want to go. You think you're in for a fast ride skyward. Step in and you're already dangling. Push the button and the cable snaps. Shut the door and you're bolting for the basement.

Trying that ride could be a new extreme sport. The Elevator Luge. Or the Psalm 37 Crash and Burn.

Want to Avoid the Elevator Luge?

Christians who find God's best have two secrets. Secret #1: They have an unquenchable desire for God's best. Secret #2: They learn wise ways to obtain their desires.

Do you want to avoid the elevator luge? Then follow God's plan. It's how you experience the extreme blessing that is already yours as a child of God. See, if you're a Christian, you already have God's unconditional acceptance and His complete approval. Because of Christ's death on the cross, you have forgiveness and stand without blame—holy—before God. If you have trusted Christ as your savior, there is not a thing you can do to make God love you more. There is nothing you could do to make Him more motivated to lead your life along His good path. But you can still get hurt if you fail to follow the path God lays out.

Life isn't happy outside God's plan. At worst, it's like an old *Batman* show: "On the wicked [God] will rain

fiery coals and burning sulfur" (Psalm 11:6). *Pow!*
"Arise, O Lord! . . . Break the teeth of the wicked"
(Psalm 3:7). *Biff!* "All sinners will be destroyed" (Psalm
37:38). *Wham!*

Sometimes it might be hard to believe God is on
duty, making sure His people win—and that evildoers
lose. But God is way ahead of you. He knows that
people have long been cooking up evil schemes to meet
their selfish needs. Remember our key verse from chapter 1? "Delight yourself in the Lord and he will give you
the desires of your heart." Well, Psalm 37:4 is sand-
wiched in a passage that shows God understands the
world in which you are trying to do life His way. He
says, "Do not fret because of evil men or be envious of
those who do wrong" (37:1). "Evil men will be cut off,
but those who hope in the Lord will inherit the land"
(37:9). "The Lord laughs at the wicked, for he knows
their day is coming" (37:13). And, "If the Lord delights
in a man's way, he makes his steps firm" (37:23). You
can give the rest of Psalm 37 a read to find out even
more about what happens when you don't stick close to
God.

So would you really want to follow your own plan for
getting what you want? Do you actually want to try
doing extreme your own way? Not really, right? Neither
do we. But living by God's way takes believing that His
way *is* best.

I want to fix in your mind what might be a new
thought: *The most extreme, fulfilling life you could ever*

live happens when you make your way into God's plan.
I can't tell you exactly what "extreme" will look like for
you, except for a promise we read a few pages back.
Read it again: " 'For I know the plans I have for you,'
declares the Lord, 'plans to prosper you and not to
harm you, plans to give you a hope and a future' " (Jeremiah 29:11).

You can make up your own plan—or you can get
into God's plan for you. You could set your own boundaries—or be wise enough to live within God's boundaries. You can rely on your own inventive, but limited,
mind, to make choices and map your life—or you can
seek God and the ways He mapped out for you, His creation.

Great Reasons to Trust God

None of us will desire God's plan if we aren't convinced His plan is for our good.

The Bible is full of great reasons to trust God. Here
are some of the best:

* *God doesn't tease you.* Scientists know that one
  way homing pigeons find home is responding
  to the earth's magnetic field. How do they
  know? They put a magnetic coil on a homing
  pigeon's head and made it so scatterbrained it
  got lost. God doesn't play those games with
  you. Remember the promise: " 'For I know the

plans I have for you,' declares the Lord, 'plans to prosper you and not to harm you, plans to give you hope and a future' " (Jeremiah 29:11).

* *God knows you best.* Your parents maybe have a fuzzy ultrasound picture of you in the womb. But God had *perfect* vision of who you would be. He saw you when He "knit you together" (Psalm 139:13). He had flawless insight into what He planned for you. Because God built you, He knows you inside and out.

* *God wants to give you rest.* Jesus said, "Come to me, all you who are weary and burdened, and I will give you rest" (Matthew 11:28). David said, "The Lord is my shepherd, I shall not be in want. He makes me lie down in green pastures, he leads me beside quiet waters, he restores my soul" (Psalm 23:1–3). God has a stash of peace He wants to share with you.

* *God gives generously.* You can find no better example of God's love than Jesus Christ. Romans 8:32 is a true statement about God's attitude toward us. It says, "He who did not spare his own Son, but gave him up for us all— how will he not also, along with him, graciously give us all things?" If God spared not His *Son*—He gave Jesus for our salvation—

then I am convinced His heart is filled with love.

✳ *God wants you to know His plan for you.* Ever had a teacher who made overwhelmingly huge assignments with ridiculously short instructions—and then graded you down when you didn't produce? God isn't like that. He wants to share His mind with you: "I will instruct you and teach you in the way you should go," He says. "I will counsel you and watch over you" (Psalm 32:8).

Where There's a Way There's a Will

If you want to experience fulfillment, you need to enter through the door of trusting obedience, accepting His care as a gift, counting on God enough to eagerly discover and do His plan. And did you catch that last verse—Psalm 32:8? God has a *way* for you to go. He has a marked *path*. A good *plan*. His set of life-giving *instructions*. But what He wants for you and from you is even more special and specific than that. God's plans are so solid and sure that the Bible calls them His *will*.

You know about wills. They detail what a person wants to happen after his or her death. It's the only time in life people have to do exactly what you want, except that you're dead so you aren't around to enjoy it.

God has a will that encompasses anything that will ever happen in your life. It's His incredible plan for you that we have been discussing all along. God's will is what He, in His infinite care and wisdom, says is the best that could happen.

Part of His will is what *He* does. God will unfailingly do what He promises to do. The other part of His will is what *you* do. It's *your* response to Him. This book is about your chance to discover *your* part in God's will. You find God's will, you find God's best for your life.

Will This Be on the Test?

Understand that there are two big areas where God shows His will. The first is *His will for all Christians.* The second is *His will just for you.* God's will for all Christians is what we can call His *universal will.* God's will specifically for you is His *specific will.*

These two areas where God shows His will are just like what happens when a good teacher assigns a huge project. A good teacher first spells out requirements that apply to the whole class, instructions each person needs to follow to succeed. This loud, bold, mass communication saves time and puts everyone on notice that the standards are meant for everyone. Yet the instructions don't stop there. A good teacher pulls students aside one by one and gives guidance that fits each student's needs, interests, and unique assignment. The teacher's goal isn't to undo the first set of instructions but to apply them individually.

When it comes to the most basic, don't-miss-them instructions for living, God has communicated loudly and clearly what He wants. People who say "What's God's plan for me?" or "How do I figure out His will?" or "What would Jesus do?" often don't realize the main portion of God's will is already revealed. Guess what? God's will is often something you don't even have to guess about. It's spelled out in the commands of Scripture for everyone to see.

You probably know the stuff I am talking about. The Bible abounds with clear commands that point you down an obvious path for life, like "Don't lie," "Don't kill," "Don't steal." Or as Jesus said, "Love God totally" and "Love others as much as you love yourself."

As we will see later, it's useless to look for God's specific will for your life until you are paying attention to His universal will. He isn't looking to tell you more if you are ignoring what you already know. When it comes to what God wants for everyone—that universal will—you don't need to pray to know it, you don't need to ask advice, you can't plead "extenuating circumstances" as an excuse for not doing it. God's will is universal and absolute.

Confused, Anyone?

Just about every time I speak I hear, "Josh, I'm just not clear on God's plan for me about . . ." and you can finish the sentence. Confusion about what God wants is a tough place to be. It's like being in a big body of water and you can't reach shore. You bob up for air once, twice, and then you go under with frustration and even panic.

But people who feel this way are well on their way to finding help. Why? Because confusion assumes *you want to know God's plan for your life.* But confusion is often not the problem. If what we have said so far is true, God has a plan that is readily available to all Christians. The real problem many people have is they question if His plan is really best. They second-guess God. They wonder if His plan will really make them happy. They miss, ignore, or misunderstand God's will because they think His plan is hard to figure out—or so scary they wouldn't want it even if they found it!

We've already learned that God *wants* you to know His plan. But even if right now you doubt your ability to discern God's will, in the pages that follow we will help you discover God's will with certainty in some of life's most vital areas.

Don't Be Muleheaded

In many, many counseling situations we find that not knowing God's will—and missing out on God's best—is the result of an unwillingness to seek and do what God desires. When each of us is drowning in confusion, it's often because we are awash in a sea of un-willingness.

That reluctance is no surprise to God. In fact, right after He promised, "I will instruct you and teach you in the way you should go; I will counsel you and watch over you" (Psalm 32:8), He warned, "Do not be like the horse or the mule, which have no understanding but must be controlled by bit and bridle or they will not come to you" (Psalm 32:9).

You don't want to fight what God wants for you. But how do you know where your heart is at? Your attitude toward God's will shows up in several ways, so see if you spot yourself:

* *"I don't really want God's will—I'm afraid of it."* You might have a wholesale fear of what God wants for you. Like the fear of what your weird aunt will give you for Christmas—yet another ugly sweater—only with bad implications as large as life. You think that God is out to ruin not only today but every day.

* *"I want part of God's plan and I'll ignore the rest."* Maybe you choose the parts of God's will you like best, reserving the right to point and pick like you are in a cafeteria line. You want the parts of God's will that sound fun and beneficial but shy away from anything that hurts or takes discipline to achieve.

* *"I want to know God's will so I can decide whether to do it."* You sound willing and teachable, but only until you know all of your options. That's like clinging to a friend only until someone better comes along. If you have this attitude, you want to stay in control. Problem? God is a lot better at being in control than we are.

* *"I can use some of God's help, but I can pretty much figure out life on my own."* Ever been in the backseat while your parents drive in circles, refusing to stop and ask directions? That's this attitude. You might think of learning everything by experience. You may find it hard to admit you need help. Either way, you miss out on God's guidance.

* *"I'm willing to do God's will whatever it is."* If you have this mind-set, you accept the goodness of where God wants to lead you even before He unfolds the road map. You trust His character and care, so you are willing to go wherever He leads. Now, that's the attitude you need if you want to find God's will—God's best for your life.

Do you see why that last approach to God's plan is the one that works? Not being sure whether you want to follow God's will is like driving a car and pushing both pedals at once. With one foot you step on the gas, asking, "God, what's your plan?" With the other foot you hit the brake and say, "I don't know whether I want to do that part of your plan." If you aren't sure that you are willing to do God's will, it will be difficult to follow it. Your attempts to go anywhere will be filled with painful starts and stops.

Strangely, sometimes you gain the extreme desires of your heart by giving up what you want and submitting to God. As you delight in Him, God has a way of fulfilling the deepest desires of your heart.

Getting Without Grabbing

You may have noticed that a lot of people assume the only way to make it in life is to wield an attitude, grab all they can, prove that they're the biggest, baddest girl or guy on the block. But God only gives to those who don't grab.

You want to live life to the extreme? Put God's will ahead of yours. Don't try to live extreme outside God's plan. God is saying, "You have to trust me. I have good things for you. I have things that are even better than your dreams." Are you ready to submit, commit, and trust God?

We might know God has a plan for our lives, and we might even want to follow it. How do we find out what His will really is? Let's figure that out.

CHAPTER 3

I Want to Love and Be Loved

Tyler and Deena have been boyfriend and girlfriend for three months.

Deena thinks their relationship is going great. Tyler is so sweet. He gets to church every Sunday now and they sit together all the way up front. Deena's parents aren't crazy about Tyler, but she thinks they'll come around. He's brought her home late a couple times, but it wasn't really his fault. Deena swears they were just talking and lost track of time. As far as Deena is concerned, the only problem with Tyler is that when she talks about God's will for their future, he's not sure the Bible applies much to relationships. He can't understand her belief in God's will or her desire—most of the time—to listen to her parents' insights.

There's one other little thing. Most of Deena's friends at church don't like Tyler either, and some can't understand why Deena dates at all. She thinks it would be great for their sake if God would shout from heaven that He likes their relationship.

Getting to Know God's Specific Will for You

Now, maybe you're sitting there and saying, "Josh, I've got other problems. I need help talking my parents into letting me use the car this weekend—and you don't know my parents. I need help with a billion decisions—yeah, maybe when to date and who to marry, but also what college to attend, what to major in, what classes to take now, what to do this summer break. That doesn't even get at the minor stuff I have to decide *this* week. I don't care about God's will for Deena, and I can smell from here that Tyler is bad for her. I don't need to know God's grand plan for the universe. I've got to know God's will for *me.*"

All right. Let's deal with that.

Guidance is no good if it doesn't fit your specific situation. If I were a young guy, I would be mighty discouraged if God said to me, "Maybe the woman of your dreams is in that flock of girls over there. Or maybe not. You figure it out."

You're saying, "Give me specifics. Right away!"

But do you know what God is saying? "Give me your heart. Right now!"

First Things First

Some people see life as a school lunch line—or better yet, as a college cafeteria with a gigantic spread of everything to eat. You know, the kind where if you eat one of everything you look like a blimp? Some foods smell irresistible to you. Others curl your nose. Overwhelmed by all the options, you wonder where to start.

But here's the thing. If life looks like a cafeteria, it's easy to think you are totally in charge of what goes on your plate. Parts of God's will you naturally like. It's obvious they are God's very best. Other parts can be harder to swallow. We talked about that in the last chapter. So you pick and choose and hope God doesn't notice you never touch the vegetables. Or fruit. Or other healthy stuff.

You can live without broccoli.

You can't thrive without the good things God wants to stack on your plate.

Whether you recognize it or not, God is in charge. Allowing Him to fill up the plate of your life is the right thing to do. But it is also rewarding. It is your first step in getting that specific advice you want—about your love life or anything else. Romans 12:1–2 says not only that you should submit to God's will, but that *submitting* is how you find the will of God! Look at this:

> Therefore, I urge you, brothers, in view of God's mercy, to offer your bodies as living sacrifices, holy and pleasing to God—this is your spiritual act of worship. Do not conform any longer to the pattern of this world, but be transformed by the renewing of your mind. Then you will be able to test and approve what God's will is—his

good, pleasing and perfect will.

Do you hear that? When you offer all of yourself to God—learning to think like He thinks and want what He wants—then "you will be able to test and approve what God's will is—his good, pleasing and perfect will."

Less-Than-Good Will

When we're honest with ourselves, we have to admit that stubbornness sometimes creeps into our hearts. There are areas where sometimes we don't always want to offer ourselves to God. We don't want Him to fill our plate. We want things our way. So daily we need to recommit to doing what we know is God's will. God has a universal will for the world, and you are included in that. Even Jesus had to consciously choose the Father's path. When He faced the cross He prayed, "Not my will, but yours be done" (Luke 22:42).

You have probably thought once or twice—okay, maybe a billion or two billion times—about what you want from a relationship with the opposite sex. Even if you feel like a total failure in getting along with girls or guys right now, you hope that someday that ravishing bride or knight in shining armor will swing your way.

Are you willing to give your whole love life to God?

If you resist God's will—His will for your love life or any other part of life—then seeking more of His will is pointless. Here's why:

✳ *You strain your relationship with God.* God leads people who trust Him. When you stop trusting you stop being led. It's like an old AM radio—or a bad audio stream on the Internet. You get static—or the connection drops altogether.

✳ *You aren't in the right place to hear from God.* In John 12:26 Jesus said, "Whoever serves me must follow me; and where I am, my servant also will be." The farther you are from God's presence, the harder it is to hear.

All of this is why I said in the last chapter that as a believer you need to make a commitment to follow God's will even before you figure it out. You get to say, "I am willing to do God's will whatever it is." That's the only attitude that works. And you know what? If you make that one huge decision to submit in all things, every other decision to go God's way is clearer and easier.

The Big Picture

And here's why giving God free rein in your life matters so much on issues of love and sex. How you handle your love life as a young person is a big test of whether you are going to follow God's clear commands. It's one of the biggest areas of life where you need specific guid-

GOD'S WILL, GOD'S BEST

ance. But you can't get to God's specifics for you without getting a grip on God's big picture for everyone.

Think about it this way: God isn't willing to point out
the girl or guy of your dreams if you're dreaming of
doing things outside His big picture.

What Kind of Guidance Do You Want From God?

Getting to God's *specific will* for something in your
life always starts by learning and loving God's big-
picture will—or *universal will*.

Since finding love for life is so incredibly important—and I am sure you put it way up on your list of top
desires—it's no surprise our Creator sets some *rules fit
for everyone*. Some *universal commands*. Some *boundaries* for its use. Here's where knowing God's will gets
easy. When it comes to God's universal will, it's never
hard to find a key verse that unlocks that area, a verse
that shows you how to delight in God and fulfill the desires of your heart. The Bible is the place to begin,
whatever your question about God's will.

I had a student come to me. He was dating this girl
and he said, "Josh, I really don't know what to do."

"What do you mean?" I asked.

"My girlfriend and I've been . . ." he said, "you
know . . . doing sexual things and stuff, and I really
don't know if it's God's will."

"You've got to be kidding," I said. "You don't have

to wonder about that! You don't even have to pray about it." Then I told him about 1 Thessalonians 4:3, which says "it is God's will that you should be sanctified: that you should avoid sexual immorality." I told him, "God's will is that you be sanctified—that you be pure. You're in a situation of sexual immorality."

And then he started to fidget. I could hear his mind grind. "Well, if that's the answer," he was thinking, "do I really want to do the will of God?" His attitude wasn't, "God, show me your will so I can do it." His attitude was, "God, show me your will so I can see if I want it."

This part of knowing God's will is so easy! You never have to ask, "Lord, is sex before marriage your will?"

What Could God Know About Love?

If God's will is what you want—if you have made the big decision that you want to pursue purity—then you're ready to hear a few more Bible teachings about God's will for the world's dating games.

You know, biology hasn't changed since Bible days, and God's best for love fits as well now as it did back then. In case you wonder if the Bible has anything relevant to say about sexuality, remember what was going on when it was written. God's people were surrounded by people who made sex a religious rite—and staffed temples with prostitutes for so-called worship. Paul's letters show that his readers had emerged from deep sexual sin, including affairs, incest, premarital sex, and homosexuality. To be honest, that sounds *worse* than what most of us face daily.

God's rules are made for the real world. Purity is meant for everyone. Check out these insights into God's universal will:

* *God is more important than any human love.* Lots of people make a boyfriend or girlfriend into a mini-god or mini-goddess. He or she determines how they spend their time or what emotional and physical boundaries they set. God says, "You shall have no other gods before me" (Exodus 20:3).

* *God made people to marry.* 1 Corinthians 7:2–3 says it's better than okay with God that people marry and keep each other content. Do you like this God or what?

* *God intends believers to partner with believers.* That's the question I hear over and over again: Should I spend time with this person or get married? First I ask if the person is a believer. If not, you can be sure that it's not God's will. You can check it out in 2 Corinthians 6:14–15.

* *Sexual fulfillment comes within marriage from your spouse.* Hebrews 13:4 says that marriage

should be honored by all and "the marriage bed kept pure." Proverbs 5:19, believe it or not, says, "May her breasts satisfy you always." That means it's God's will for married couples to be faithful to each other.

✴ *Sexual sin starts in the mind.* Real purity isn't just right actions but right thoughts. Your real attitude about love is seen in where your eyes and heart wander when no one is looking. Jesus said in Matthew 5:28 that "anyone who looks at a woman lustfully has already committed adultery with her in his heart."

Checking Your Heart

Those are all parts of God's universal will. God says other things in Scripture that begin to point you toward His specific will for you. But before I get to those, I want to ask a pointed question: How are you doing in following God's universal will for your love life?

From elementary school on, Molly had a string of boys following her. By the time she was sixteen, a boy convinced her he was the love of her life and she became sexually active. Even though a few years later Molly became a Christian and even entered Christian ministry, her past haunted her. She endlessly compared her new husband to guys she had been with and guys she met at work. Two divorces later, she still struggles to submit her love life to God.

If you don't control your behavior, your relationship could end up being built on the wrong foundation. If you don't control your thoughts, your wrong thoughts could end up controlling your behavior. God won't bless that.

If you struggle in this area, keep reading. Don't give up. But allow God to bring your thoughts and life in line with His will on the big issues first. See, if you are not experiencing and wanting to do God's universal will—what He wants for everyone—then why would God divulge details for your individual situation? You say, "Ooo, that makes it rough." No, it doesn't. It makes it honest. You might be thinking, "This is serious." It is. Love is complicated. It's intense. It's for keeps. It can ruin your life or make it a riot. That's why you need to know and obey God's universal will before you look for His specific will.

You Don't Worship the Easter Bunny

Some people confuse God and the Easter Bunny. They picture God scattering knowledge of His will all over the place, hiding it behind rocks and bushes so it's hard to find. It's good stuff to get, but if you don't, too bad. It's all a game.

God doesn't play games. God loves you enough to be interested in the details of your life, even your pursuit of true love. He isn't aiming to hide anything. Without a doubt, He has a will for your life and wants you to know it.

Why? First, God cares incredibly for you. Second, that care extends to having a moment-by-moment will for your life. God has a will for each activity of your day. God has a will for each day of the week, each week of the month, and each month of the year. In Matthew 6: 26 it says, "Look at the birds of the air; they do not sow or reap or store away in barns, and yet your heavenly Father feeds them." Matthew 10:29 and 31 tell us: "Are not two sparrows sold for a penny? Yet not one of them will fall to the ground apart from the will of your Father. . . . You are worth more than many sparrows." If God makes dinner reservations and flight plans for every sparrow on earth, God without a doubt has a will for every second of your existence.

Unlocking God's Specific Will for Your Love Life

Is God going to pick the person you should develop a relationship with right now? Will you find a note from God tomorrow morning in your locker telling you who to marry eight or ten years from now?

First, it's good to know that God won't force you into a relationship you don't want. He won't walk you to the altar in a straitjacket. The whole counsel of Scripture shows that God respects your free will.

Second, whatever guidance God gives, you still have

to live the choice. Love is a decision, not a dungeon. And you might have noticed—a relationship requires that someone else likes you as much as you like them.

And third, relationships are huge decisions. You need to access all the ways God guides you. In this book we will cover four basic ways to discover God's guidance, ways you can use whatever the decision you face. You might think of it as a four-step strategy for knowing God's will:

You need *prayer*.

You need *counsel*.

You need to understand your *circumstances*.

But first you need *Scripture*.

God's Light for Your Path

Scripture is the first place you start when you want to know God's universal will. It is also the first place to go to know God's specific will, your first step in that four-part strategy for finding God's best for you. Scripture teaches that we have a great resource available to us in making personal decisions. Paul wrote that "all Scripture is inspired by God and is useful to teach us what is true and to make us realize what is wrong in our lives. It straightens us out and teaches us to do what is right" (2 Timothy 3:16 NLT). Generations of Christians will testify that "[God's] word is a lamp to my feet and a light for my path" (Psalm 119:105).

When you read the Bible for God's specific guidance,

you want to ask yourself, "What does this verse mean?" It isn't a case of "this verse *isn't* for me" but "this one is *especially* for me."

When you read Scripture regularly, you often find a verse that nails your situation, hits you between the eyes, speaks right to your need. You may have heard about "God's still, small voice." Isaiah 30:21 says that "whether you turn to the right or to the left, your ears will hear a voice behind you, saying, 'This is the way; walk in it.'" God's voice speaks in the language of Scripture, and as you read more and more of the Bible you are learning God's language, learning to hear His quiet leading specifically for your life.

So where do you start? Since you probably aren't getting married tomorrow, start with what Paul says about the benefits of singleness (1 Corinthians 7:7–9) and being content in every situation (Philippians 4:11–12). Look at verses that tell you to set your love life expectations high (1 Corinthians 13; Proverbs 31:10–31). Remind yourself that beauty is only skin deep (Proverbs 31:30; 1 Timothy 2:9–10; 1 Samuel 16:7). Study the love stories of the Bible, both good and bad—David and Bathsheba (2 Samuel 11–12), Samson and Delilah (Judges 16), Ruth and Boaz (Ruth 2–4), and Joseph and Mary (Matthew 1:18–25). Take to heart what the Bible says about staying in control (Ephesians 4:17–24; Galatians 5:22–25) and testing everything you do against the motivation of glorifying God (1 Corinthians 10:31).

And read passages that remind you God invented romance (Proverbs 5:15–19; 30:18–19).

So I Read Those. What Now?

If you read all those verses, will you know God's total will for your love life?

No. But it's a start.

The Bible sets boundaries for your life. It tells you a lot about how to navigate life within those boundaries. But getting God's specific guidance isn't always as simple as reading every verse in the Bible on a topic. God has designed other ways to show you His will, things I mentioned above—prayer, counsel, and circumstances. He uses those methods to guide you as well.

Step by Step

One more thing.

The Bible makes it exceedingly clear that God not only has a will and wants you to seek it, but He also wants to tell you what that will is. Remember Psalm 32: 8? God says, "I will instruct you and teach you in the way you should go; I will counsel you and watch over you." Many Christians read a verse like that and think, "Huh? What instruction? What counsel? I've never seen God dispense advice like the guidance office does at school. If that's what you mean, I don't think I've ever had the counsel of God. I go through day after day after day without knowing what God wants of me."

You have already seen how God reveals much of what you need to know in life through His *universal* will. You don't need to pray about it. You don't need to ask for opinions about it. You just need to do it. You have also seen how Scripture is the first place to go to know God's *specific* will just for you.

But here's that one more thing: *Discovering God's will takes time.* I won't promise you a once-for-all, good-for-the-rest-of-your-life discovery of God's will, because that isn't how God works.

God isn't going to tell you everything right now, and detecting His specific will is an ongoing process. Don't be frustrated that you have to work at it. God usually leads you little by little, keeping you close to Him. He counts on you to walk step by step in relationship with Him and learn from Him—because after all, finding your heart's desire is all about delighting in *Him.*

CHAPTER 4

I Want to Be Surrounded by God's Friends

Friends are a *doubly* powerful presence in your life. Not only can they fill the emotional needs of the heart, but here's the doubly powerful part: The right companions also propel you toward all the rest of God's best. That should make you happy—doubly happy. That makes friends really important.

You know that friends matter, but here's an easy way to tell how much. Take this five-second quiz: What's the first thing you do when you walk into your school lunchroom?

Tick. Tick. Tick. Tick. Tick.

Time's up. The first real thing you do is *look for friends.* One glance tells you who to sit with. You know where you are welcome—and where you are not.

No matter where you go, what matters most— almost always—is whether you have friends with you. You might be wired to want a lot of friends, or you might be content with one or two. You might get withdrawal unless you're with them all the time, or you might need a lot of your own space. You might even count your family among your best friends, because your family was, after all, your *first* set of friends.

Not that friends make anyone's life perfect. You surely know what it's like to have friendships go sour. You know how it feels not to belong. You lock yourself in your room. You turn on some music. And sometimes music can help. But listening to CDs or the radio for too long can be a dead end. That world between your head-phones gets pretty tiny after a while, doesn't it?

That's because God never meant you to go through life alone.

Sketch Me the Perfect Friend

You don't just need any old friends, though. You need the *right* friends.

Think of the friends you have right now. What makes them friends worth having? What do you need from them? You don't want friends who forget you. You would like people to do more than tolerate you. You need something better than a crew of neutral non-enemies.

You could easily make a list or draw a picture of everything you want in a friend and talk on for hours about it. Whether you feel like you have a lot of friends or a few, you know all about them. The Bible has many illustrations of friends—good and bad—starting way back at the beginning of human history:

✳ *Adam and Eve* were the world's first friends, but their oldest son killed his brother (Genesis 4:8).

✳ *Ruth* formed such a strong friendship with her mother-in-law, *Naomi*, that she stayed with her in a far-off country even after Ruth's husband died (Ruth 1:16).

✳ *David and Jonathan* became unselfish allies despite the fact that Jonathan's father, Saul, tried to kill David (1 Samuel 18).

✳ *Jesus* knew what it was to be betrayed and rejected. "He came to that which was his own, but his own did not receive him" (John 1:11). And He was handed over to die by *Judas*, a close follower (Matthew 26:49–50).

✳ The *friends of a paralyzed man* ripped a hole in a roof and lowered him in to be healed by Jesus (Mark 2:1–5).

✳ The *early church* was close and "gave to anyone as he had need" (Acts 2:45).

✳ *James* instructed Christians to be accountable to one another (James 5:16).

✷ *Paul* warned against believers who "bite and devour" one another (Galatians 5:15).

✷ The book of Revelation shows *God's people* living together in God's presence for all eternity (Revelation 21:3–4).

One last one: When Jesus said that the two most important commands in all of the Bible are to love God and love others (Luke 10:27), you can be sure that God has put relationships at the center of the universe.

What you likely want from your friends—and what God wants for you—is *belonging*.

But to be honest, not everyone finds true love with that one dream guy or girl and lives happily ever after. Yet that doesn't mean you don't find true friendship. God wants you to have true friends. It's His will. Yet you need to understand how that happens.

The Things You Do for Love

Some Christians think spiritual maturity means you can get along on your own—just Jesus and me going down life's open road. But belonging to God never takes away your need for people. You have an inescapable longing for *human* belonging.

There is no shortage of ways to belong.

✷ There are *bad ways to belong*. You know about

gangs—a surrogate family where membership might leave you dead. Or the party crowd—"friends" who race to the end of a case of beer. That way of belonging gets you a warped brand of acceptance that can lead to destruction.

* There are *snobby ways to belong*. Cliques are igloos—toasty on the inside, frigid on the outside. Cliques can be held together by good things or bad things. But it's never easy to get in—assuming you want to.

* There are *weird ways to belong*. The MTV show *Real World* dumps guys and girls in a house to live together and find out more about one another than anyone ever needs to know. It's not much different from the guys camping permanently in girlfriends' rooms—or vice versa—that goes on in college dorms, situations a lot like living in a sexual sewer.

God has a *better way to belong*.

2 Timothy 2:22 Friends

"Everything bad I ever learned to do I learned at church," says Emily. "My friends' favorite place to smoke pot was under the steps at church. On retreats, girls and guys paired off and did everything but every-thing. Last summer the high school choir from church toured South Dakota. They wound up in a street brawl at the Corn Palace. I went on a summer missions trip to Appalachia instead. It was the first time I'd seen *real* Christians my age. They lived what they believed. They were the first really helpful friends I'd ever had, and meeting them totally changed my life."

What a world of difference between Emily's two sets of friends! You can be surrounded by friends—even church friends—and totally miss the incredible rela-tionships God intends for you.

God's will is for you to have close friends who help you get closer to Him. You can call them "2 Timothy 2: 22 friends," because that's the verse that describes them: "Flee the evil desires of youth, and pursue right-eousness, faith, love and peace, *along with those who call on the Lord out of a pure heart*" (italics added). Those "along with" people are *good* friends. They are *Christian* friends. They are *good Christian* friends.

God's best friends help you steer clear of trouble. They help you pursue God's best for your life. Together, out of pure hearts, you call on the Lord. Finding those 2 Timothy 2:22 friends is the only way to meet the de-sire of your heart for belonging.

The Need for Friendship

You might not be so sure those are the friends you want.

Mitch's parents wanted him to make Christian friends so badly that they told him to invite anyone he wanted to church socials—even to pricey retreats—as their treat. Mitch wasn't swayed. "I don't want church friends!" he yelled. "Have you ever seen those kids? They're as lame as they get. They sing songs and hold hands and *blech*. What more do you need to know?"

God isn't like parents who wish you would build strong friendships with solid peers so they don't stare at the ceiling all night long worrying about what you're doing. God knows even more than your parents about the hazards of having the wrong friends. And He knows infinitely more about the good things good friends will lead you into. Remember? Friends are doubly powerful. Not only do they meet your need for friendship, but the right companions pull you toward all the other things God wills for your life.

In fact, the Bible says Christian friends are your lifeblood. You probably know what the Bible says in 1 Corinthians 12 about believers being the body of Christ, how we are all like different body parts and can't get along without one another. A foot can't say, "Because I'm not a hand, I don't belong to the body." That doesn't stop the foot from being part of the whole. An ear can't say, "Because I'm not an eye, I'm going to quit hearing." But what happens to an eye or an ear or a finger detached from the body? It quickly dies. It dries up. It disintegrates into dust and blows away.

Having Christian friends isn't an optional good idea.

It's a basic need. Having Christian friends isn't about staying warm and huge. It's about survival.

So What Do Christian Friends Do?
Be Together

God wants you to "flee the evil desires of youth, and pursue righteousness, faith, love and peace, along with those who call on the Lord out of a pure heart." All of that starts with the "along with." And 2 Timothy 2:22 friends don't just happen. You have got to get together. Fact is, you have to *make time* to *make friends* and *make sure your friendships are on track.*

"I had friends at my public high school," a college student recalls. "But my closest friends were at church. We had interests in common, but most of all we had Jesus at the center of our relationships. We saw each other in the middle of the week for Bible study, on Sunday for services, and once or twice more just to be together. Because of my experience of those great relationships, I knew what kind of growing Christian friends to look for when I went to school. I know I can't live without them."

The Bible has a concrete test to tell whether your life is in line with God's plan: "Let us not give up meeting together, as some are in the habit of doing" (Hebrews 10:25). I know that might be a hard one to hear. Are you in the habit of getting together with Christian friends? God's universal will is that you *be together* with other Christians.

So What Do Christian Friends Do?
Act Together

When Paul talks about those "evil desires of youth" you should avoid, why do you think he singles out *youth*? Well, the person who received his letter—Timothy—was still young. In an earlier letter to Timothy, Paul wrote, "Don't let anyone look down on you because you are young, but set an example for the believers" (1 Timothy 4:12). Paul had great expectations for Timothy, not great fears.

Even so, Paul knew that as a younger person Timothy faced powerful temptations that could trip him up. So he shared a secret of staying spiritually strong. Paul's words mean Timothy should "flee and keep on fleeing" the evil desires of youth. He also must "pursue and keep on pursuing" God's good will. And he should do those things not just alone but *along with* other believers.

Don't just *be* together, the verse is saying. *Act together.*

The whole Bible is a manual on how to team up and have encouraging Christian friendships. But here Paul makes it simple. Flee one thing: evil. And chase four things:

❋ *Righteousness*. God's purity. Relying solely on Christ's death for your sins for your right standing with God.

❋ *Faith*. A well-founded trust in God.

❋ *Love*. Wanting and doing the best for other people.

❋ *Peace*. Harmonious relationships.

You need to be together with other believers so you can *act together*. You can flee what is evil: "Encourage one another daily . . . so that none of you may be hardened by sin's deceitfulness," says Hebrews 3:13. You can pursue what is good: "Let us consider how we may spur one another on toward love and good deeds," says Hebrews 10:24.

So What Do Christian Friends Do?
Pray Together

You might *be together* with Christian friends. Maybe you *act together*. To *pray together* consistently could be harder for you. Yet prayer is the indispensable "call on the Lord out of a pure heart" part of 2 Timothy 2:22. Look at some of the places where the phrase "call on" shows up in Scripture to see what it means:

* Back at the very beginning of the Bible: "Seth also had a son, and he named him Enosh. At that time men began to *call on* the name of the Lord" (Genesis 4:26).

* When Elijah needed God to defeat some false prophets: "Then you [the false prophets] *call on* the name of your god, and I [Elijah] will *call on* the name of the Lord. The god who answers by fire—he is God" (1 Kings 18:24).

* In an everyday request for help: "I *call on* the Lord in my distress, and he answers me" (Psalm 120:1).

* When people place their trust in Christ and become Christians: "Everyone who *calls on* the name of the Lord will be saved" (Romans 10: 13).

To "call on" means to speak your need, turning your dependence on God into prayer. In Matthew 18: 19–20 Jesus specifically promised to be present with you when you are praying with another believer.

And prayer is exactly how God really uses your friends to propel you into all that He has for you. That is the part of friendship that makes it a doubly powerful desire.

Grabbing Hold of God's Plan

It is God's universal, no-doubt-about-it will that you *be together* with other believers. That you *act together*. And that you *pray together*. You can pray for all sorts of things. In fact, part of God's universal will is that you "pray continually" (1 Thessalonians 5:17).

You also have the privilege of praying together to ask God to lead you into His specific will.

See, your first step in discovering God's will is found in the Bible. What has God said that fits everyone? And what has God said that specially fits your situation? Look for relevant Scriptures. Start applying them to your life. But even as you search for insight into God's specific will, start to pray. That's the second part of our four-step strategy for uncovering God's best. Praying for wisdom is your God-given mechanism for inviting God to be Lord of your life and of a specific situation. Prayer is how you ask for God's will to be done in your heart as it is in heaven. Prayer lets you speak up, to declare your commitment to God, and to ask for the guidance God is so eager to give.

And this is exciting: *You don't have to pray alone!*

Make a list of things that you want to know God's will for in your life. Pray for them on your own. But it is immensely helpful to find someone else who will pray with you. Maybe just for four or five minutes a day—pray with your friend, your father, your mother, your sister, your brother. All you have to do is say, "These are things I need to know God's will on. Will you get together with me to pray?" It's amazing what God will show you when you ask.

Acts 13:2–3 is a great example of an answer to prayer for guidance. As the early church prayed, God revealed His will to them for that situation. Everyone knew the right thing to do. Prayer is God's great gift for understanding His will.

Taking Hold of God's Plan Together

Praying together for God's will through the big issues of life is a great privilege.

Christ's loneliest moment on earth came at the cross. As He thought about the spiritual and physical pain that lay ahead, He shook in prayer. Remember in the Garden of Gethsemane? He was heading toward the cross, and He cried out, "If it be possible, let this cup be taken from me. Let the crucifixion be taken from me. However, *your will* be done." See, more than not going through the suffering and pain was His desire to follow God's will. And how did He know it? Through prayer.

Jesus was extremely committed to His Father's will. He struggled to the point of sweating blood (Luke 22: 44). What Jesus wanted, though, was friends to pray with Him. Maybe you recall when He was praying and He had asked his closest friends to pray with Him. But they went to sleep instead (Matthew 26:36–45).

You have the chance to stay alert and pray with

friends as they struggle to figure out, accept, and do God's will. You start by praying for God's guidance, taking hold of God's plan through prayer. Then you pray for the things you discern to be God's will. That's being persistent together through prayer. And finally you pray until you see your prayers answered or until God persuades you that you misunderstood His will. You can pray for health. Relationships. School. Family battles. Money for genuine needs. Leisure. Spiritual growth. You can pray for *all* the desires of your heart that honor God.

Show Me the Friends, Josh

"This all sounds nice," you might be thinking, "but I don't have anyone. I don't have any 2 Timothy 2:22 friends in my life. I've tried. They aren't there."

There may not be a quick or easy answer to that pain. But know one thing: God knows your problem and will work with you to solve it.

"My first year at a public university my roommate became a Christian," Teresa shared. "I thought, well, that was easy. I'll do that again. So the next year at another school I again played roommate roulette and was assigned a roommate by the school. That year, my roommate wanted nothing to do with God. By midyear I was dying for Christian support. I wound up moving off campus to live in a small house of Christians. The girls there weren't my first choices for friends, but at that point I knew I needed closeness with people who shared my faith."

Sometimes new Christian friends are easy to make. That is what Teresa saw happen her first year in college. But sometimes you might struggle to find friends, and in that struggle you learn to cling to God. In Psalm 73 David cries out in loneliness and yet comes to this conclusion: "Whom have I in heaven but you? And earth has nothing I desire besides you. My flesh and my heart may fail, but God is the strength of my heart and my portion forever" (Psalm 73:25–26). For those times when you feel incredibly alone, you can remember that God himself is there for you. That's what Jesus found out in the Garden of Gethsemane when His friends slept.

And when you delight in God, He gives you the desire of your heart.

Especially when it comes to true Christian friends.

See, God doesn't want you to live your faith alone. When Elijah complained to God that he was the only faithful person left in Israel and some people were about to kill him, God comforted him. And then God reminded him, "Elijah, I have *seven thousand* other people in Israel who are faithful to me. Let me show you where they are" (see 1 Kings 19:1–18). Immediately afterward, God paired Elijah with Elisha, who carried on Elijah's job as a prophet.

When you feel alone, ask God to show you some of those seven thousand people who radically follow Him.

Ask God for 2 Timothy 2:22 friends. And ask Him to show you how you can *make time* to *make friends* and *make sure your friendships are on track.*

That's the only way to get those doubly powerful friends in your life.

CHAPTER 5

I Want a Meaningful Career

Fast forward your life a couple decades. You are at work, staring at the clock ticking . . . in . . . slow . . . motion.

You thought that once you graduated from high school your clock-watching days were over forever. But suddenly you are thirty-five or fortyish, and you look just like your mom or dad, and turning forty-five or fifty suddenly doesn't seem so far off, and you wonder where the years went, and you dread thirty . . . more . . . years . . . of staring at the clock on your cubicle wall.

The sound of a closing door interrupts your stare. It's 7:43 P.M. Your boss left, so you can finally leave. Time to escape—until tomorrow morning, that is.

Thirty-Six Million Seconds of Your Life

Do you remember the antidrug TV ads about how no one ever expects to grow up into a drug addict? Well, no kid ever plans to have an unbelievably boring job either. Whether you expect to work a "normal" job someday, to stay at home and care for your kids, to start your own business, or to dream up some work arrangement not yet invented, those daily eight-to-five blocks from age twenty-two to sixty-seven add up to more than 36 million seconds of life. That's a lot of clock watching, unless you are so excited about what you do that you don't care about the clock.

If you don't find a job that you're happy with, work can be a curse. It can reduce you to a cubicle dweller, a donut-inhaling middle manager, or a human droid inserting thingy part A into thingy part B until you get a repetitive stress injury and start muttering to yourself.

You probably have given up on your dream of being a baseball player or a ballerina. You might have no idea what you want to do with your life. If you are like three out of five American youth, you already have a part-time headstart in the world of work. You want those 36 million adult moments to matter—to mean something. It's a desperate desire of your heart.

Who Is Your Boss Going to Be?

As you sit in the school guidance office taking vocational aptitude tests or thumbing through an index of jobs or searching catalogs of colleges or tech schools, you aren't hoping for dull adulthood. You never ask yourself, "Where could I really waste my life? How could I flush my future? What nasty job could I get trapped in until I die?" You are concerned about what you would enjoy.

Some people might teach you that God wants to lead people into jobs they don't like or don't do well so He can teach them to be real servants. But that's not how God leads you to find your life's work.

A good place to start could be to ask: "*What* do I like?" But if you want to find God's will for your work life, there is an even more basic question: *Whom* do you want for your boss? Sooner or later you will be a part-time professional something or other. And if you will spend 36 million of the best seconds of your life in some kind of labor, wouldn't you want to work for the best boss in the world?

You probably are up to your eyeballs in homework—and you might go on to flip burgers, compile spreadsheets, head a company, or run the country. Whatever you do, you can have the best boss in the world. Because you can work for God himself. Colossians 3:23 says, "Whatever you do, work at it with all your heart, as working for the Lord, not for men."

Get it? If you delight in God, if you decide that *He* is your ultimate employer, then *who you work for* is even more important than *what you do* in keeping your heart happy. Because God can make any kind of work more than a job.

Cosmic Career Planning

That said, what you do *is* incredibly important. God is like any good boss. He does some cosmically wise career planning. With God, there is no such thing as a wasted life. There is no such thing as a dead end. Working for God makes every moment of your working life matter.

God knows all about the curse of work. It is, in fact, part of the consequence of human sin. Back at the start of Scripture, God put Adam and Eve in the Garden of Eden. When Adam and Eve disobeyed God, they were separated from God and had to leave the garden. Instead of having a lush forest of fruit to pick from, they had to till the ground: "Cursed is the ground because of you," God told Adam. "Through painful toil you will eat of it. . . . It will produce thorns and thistles for you. . . . By the sweat of your brow you will eat your food" (Genesis 3:17–19).

Does that sound like a lousy day at work or what?

You know what that kind of day is like. It's like when your boss threatens to fire you because you dropped a burger on the floor or your teacher falls asleep reading your English essay.

For Christians, though, the curse isn't the end of the story on work. See, when you are a Christian, God has a whole lifetime of better work planned for you. Read this: "For it is by grace you have been saved, through faith—and this not from yourselves, it is the gift of

God—not by works, so that no one can boast. For we are God's workmanship, created in Christ Jesus to do good works, which God prepared in advance for us to do" (Ephesians 2:8–10). You are God's "workmanship"—literally translated, his "poem" or "work of art." He has planned your life in advance. It's a life of good works.

Ephesians 2:8–10 is specific about how God acts in Christ to save you. But it's about all of life. And it absolutely applies to those 36 million potentially boring seconds of working life. So understand what it means: God has given you a relationship with himself by grace, through faith—in other words, as a gift, not because of anything good you did. Now that you are His friend through Christ Jesus, He is going to let you in on all kinds of wonderful things to do.

But there is only one way to get in on God's career planning: You need to let Him lead you where He wants you to go.

But Won't God Make Me Be a Missionary?

By now you know that the truest, deepest desires of your heart come to you when you delight in God. So you have decided to live your extreme life His way. You have given Him your lips. You are trusting Him for 2 Timothy 2:22 friends.

You still might resist, however, at giving God your job. You might be reluctant to trust Him with all that time. You might wonder about letting God set your salary.

Actually, many students worry that God is going to make them a pastor. Or a missionary. Go on a short-term mission trip? Fine. Do a weekend work project? Great. Pursue a career in missions? No way.

Whatever you fear God might *make* you be, relax.

Yes, God is Master. He has the right to ask you to do whatever He wills. But what God asks you to do He gives you strength to do. He gifts some people to be pastors. He gifts others to be missionaries. He gifts others to do millions of other things.

More than that, wherever God leads you He works through your will. He gives you a desire that burns from the inside out. God is not likely to force you to do anything you don't want to do. God doesn't push people into ministry. While God never said, "I'm going to send you where you don't want to go," he does say, "Whom shall I send? And who will go?" (Isaiah 6:8).

Getting From Here to There

Once you decide that all the seconds of your day and all those 36 million seconds of your adult life belong to God, you still need to find your way into His will. Whether you are looking for your first part-time job or signing on the dotted line for a more long-term job, God has a lot to say about the way to do work.

You have already heard God's number one command for the world of work, Colossians 3:23: "Whatever you do," from homework to summer jobs to full-time careers, "work at it with all your heart, as working for the Lord, not for men." Here's more on how you work for the Lord in real life.

Step 1: Study God's Universal Will for Work

God's universal, made-for-everyone will is that every second of work you do would be

* *Honest*. In Amos 8:5–6 God condemns merchants known for "skimping the measure, boosting the price and cheating with dishonest scales, buying the poor with silver and the needy for a pair of sandals, selling even the sweepings with the wheat." In case you weren't sure, being a drug dealer, a crooked lawyer, or a cheating businessperson is outside God's plan.

* *Diligent*. "The sluggard craves and gets nothing," says Proverbs 13:4, "but the desires of the diligent are fully satisfied."

* *Efficient*. Here's a checkup for your day planner from Ephesians 5:16–17 (NLT): "Make the most of every opportunity for doing good in these evil days. Don't act thoughtlessly, but try

to understand what the Lord wants you to do."

* *Self-supporting.* Some students go from being totally dependent on their parents at age fifteen to totally self-supporting at nineteen. Others are well funded far longer. Whatever the rules in your family and the timing of your financial independence, in adulthood God intends for you to earn your keep: "If a man will not work, he shall not eat" (2 Thessalonians 3: 10).

* *Without greed.* Money can't be the only thing that motivates your work. Colossians 3:5 calls greed "idolatry," and the Bible says this about overenthusiasm for cold hard cash: "For the love of money is a root of all kinds of evil. Some people, eager for money, have wandered from the faith and pierced themselves with many griefs" (1 Timothy 6:10).

* *Respectable.* Work either earns respect for your faith or destroys it. God's goal is that "your daily life may win the respect of outsiders" (1 Thessalonians 4:12).

* *Consistent.* "Slaves," Paul wrote, "obey your earthly masters in everything; and do it, not only when their eye is on you and to win their

favor, but with sincerity of heart and reverence for the Lord" (Colossians 3:22).

That last passage—directed to slaves, who were more like people who worked in exchange for food and housing than what a slave was in America—shows that God expects you to throw yourself into work whatever your situation.

Step 2: Surrender Your Way to Him

Letting God be master over my career choice was a huge struggle for me. When I enrolled in college and a teacher told me I was a "straight D" student, I decided to prove her and everyone else wrong. I laid out a series of goals for my life that led through law school and local political service, culminating in a plan to be governor of Michigan, my home state, in twenty-five years.

But when I became a Christian I wondered if God would derail my plans and force me to go into ministry. I discovered, though, that once I surrendered my career and said, "Whatever you want, God, I want!" then I *wanted* to be in ministry.

Now, you might be called by God to be a pilot or a pianist or a programmer or a stay-at-home parent. You won't be sure of God's path for your life, though, until you tell God you are ready to do His will.

Step 3: Recognize That Your Gifts Come From Him and Are Used for Him

Did you know that all the talents and other gifts you have come from God? He gives you those gifts, and He wants you to use them not just for yourself but for Him and for the betterment of your world. First Peter 4:10–11 says, "Each one should use whatever gift he has received to serve others . . . so that in all things God may be praised through Jesus Christ."

While that passage talks specifically about spiritual gifts, the principle applies to other gifts: God doesn't want you to waste what He gives you.

Step 4: Make Use of Scripture, Prayer, Counsel, and Circumstances

Like in any other huge decision, what you discern to be God's specific will for you isn't likely to come just from one source of guidance. You will need to use the whole four-part strategy we've been talking about. *Scripture* sets the boundaries of God's will. *Prayer* invites God to show His will. When it comes to a career, getting sound advice is especially crucial. *Counsel*, discussed below, is your third way to get God's guidance. And the *circumstances* of your life help you see God leading you through open and shut doors. More about that in the next chapter.

Good counselors make you smart. Proverbs 19:20

says, "Listen to advice and accept instruction, and in the end you will be wise." Proverbs 15:22 adds, "Plans fail for lack of counsel, but with many advisers they succeed." Your goal in hooking up with any counselor is to find someone who *knows more than you*, not someone who simply *agrees with you*. You aren't trying to figure out what *they* think you should do, but where *God* wants to lead you. Much as you want them to, the best counselors don't tell you what to do. They provide a place for you to wrestle and offer either a caution or a confirmation to what you are deciding.

You might be thinking, "Well, I've tried that and it didn't work very well." Or "I don't know how to pick a counselor." Here's how to find good counsel.

Seeking Spiritual Counsel

It's like this. You and a pack of fellow hikers come up against a sheer rock fault a dozen feet high. Your friends are the people at the bottom. They support you. Boost you. Pray with you. Lift you as far as they can to help you climb up. The people at the top are trained counselors, parents, or wise people in the world of work. They make the climb so much easier because they are already where you want to go. They don't shove you from below. They grab your hands and help you from above.

Getting good counsel is getting hold of the strength

of many minds. It's gaining wisdom you don't have. Look at how it helps:

* *Counsel gives you vision for what you can be.* Many people only begin to discover how they are gifted when they get feedback from others. You might have incredible vision for a certain career, but other people can help you consider whether your gifts match up to that career.

* *Counsel steadies you.* Sometimes we can get so emotional in making a decision that our emotions cloud God's wisdom. Counsel helps us look at a question objectively.

* *Counsel gives you wisdom you don't have.* Look at your life in high school. You may have had a boss or two. It helps to talk to people who have had ten or twenty bosses. Or to vocational counselors who have seen a thousand bosses in action. Counselors have done what you haven't—picked a school, a major, looked for a first full-time job, relocated away from family, etc. Counsel helps you hurdle the wall of inexperience.

Sometimes we think we can figure everything out by ourselves. But we really can't. Listen to Proverbs 12:15: "The way of a fool seems right to him, but a wise man listens to advice." As right as our own view of a situation might seem, we need to see things through even wiser people's eyes.

Finding Wise Guys and Gals

Not every advice-giver offers good counsel, not even when he or she is a sincere Christian. "Some Christian friends who knew of my interest in missions encouraged me to major in anthropology so I could understand the cultures I would work with," Natalie explains. "But things didn't turn out how I expected. When several opportunities to go to the mission field turned into closed doors, I discerned God's will was for me to help people get to the mission field instead of going myself. I stayed home for several years with my kids, but now that my kids are in school I'm not equipped to find a good part-time career. I wish I had talked to other people who might have suggested I major in something I could do both at home and on the field. No one helped me think through all the possibilities, and I was too young to know better."

Like Natalie, you can be led off course if your counselors aren't competent. You have several sets of counselors in your life. Each offers a different slant on your life:

* *Peers.* Good friends help you get honest about who you are and how you feel, because they

see you at school, church, social situations, even work. The closer peers are to you, though, the less objective they might be. The farther away they are from you, the less they might really know you. Whether they want to help you or not, peers might not be completely honest. The support and prayers of your peers, though, is priceless.

* *School*. Homework and tests and projects are like daily feedback on what you like and dislike. Teachers and counselors can offer objective feedback on your academic abilities. Few adults at school, though, know the big nonstudent part of you. They also might not necessarily share your values and might not understand your impulse to servanthood and sacrifice.

* *Pastors*. Your pastor will likely have as much concern that you walk in God's plan as you could wish for. Ask him or her for help in setting up a small group of students to study God's will.

* *Mentors*. Mentors are experts who can coach you in a specific area. While they won't be there for you with day-to-day support and prayer like a friend, they offer specialized, one-

of-a-kind experience. Like adults at school, they probably won't know the total you. By the way, look around for some long-distance heroes. You can learn lots from people you never meet.

* *Parents*. Whether you admit it or not, even whether you get along fabulously or not, parents often know you better than anyone else. One problem: Parents aren't always objective either—they might see you as the baby who can do no wrong, or the renegade who can do no right. Ask them to talk straight with you, and try hard to hear them.

There is another point about parents that is key, yet a lot of people like to ignore it. Ephesians 6:1 says "Obey your parents." Obedience to your parents is part of God's universal will. And God often shows His specific will through your parents. And if you aren't obedient, that channel of God's will is interrupted. Big mistake.

Obedience to parents doesn't cover decisions you make when you are forty-five. But it is tremendously relevant to your choices right now. "I had done extremely well in high school," Jerome says. "I wanted to travel—forever. My parents felt I should go to college. I did get to travel later, and God has led me through a series of increasingly great jobs I never would have gotten without solid academic training. I get a pit in my stomach when I think I might have missed God's will if I hadn't listened to my parents."

Your parents might not be Christians. But all parents have been around the block once or twice. Your parents might seem too busy. But no parent has ever turned down a request to share their wisdom.

Putting Counsel to the Test

A friend of mine in his early thirties was asked to a one-to-one lunch the other day by a corporate recruiter. The recruiter offered my friend a position where he could soon be making half a million dollars a year.

That might sound like a dream—except that my friend knew enough to politely decline the offer, though he did think about it for quite a while. While lots of people give advice and even make offers to you, the ones to listen to are those who *know you best* and *want your best.* My friend's spouse and friends dragged him back to reality by pointing out that the proposed position was totally outside his lifelong passions, no matter the financial rewards.

Counsel isn't perfect. No advice is above checking and double-checking. Test it against Scripture. Pray about it to God. See what other counselors say. You have your own mind to make up.

See how wise you are getting? You are putting together that four-part process of how to discover God's best and fulfill the desires of your heart. You have heard about Scripture, prayer, and counsel. There's more to learn—from circumstances—as we look at living large in the next chapter.

CHAPTER 6

I Want the Good Life

B y the 1870s scientists had worked for many years to devise an electric light. One of them, Thomas Edison, sent assistants to Japan and the Amazon jungle to examine more than six thousand types of vegetation—hickory, cedar, flax, bamboo—for use as his filament, the wire in a bulb that makes light when electricity flows through it. After conducting twelve hundred experiments—tests more complicated than any he had ever done—Edison succeeded. In 1879 a light bulb using a filament of carbonized cotton sewing thread burned for two days.

The light bulb was only one of Edison's 1,093 patented inventions. He invented

* *an automatic telegraph* sending and receiving machine

* a transmitter that made Alexander Bell's *phone* usable

* the *phonograph*, first using a tinfoil cylinder, then a disk

* *alkaline batteries*, the result of many thousands of experiments

* the world's first large central electric *power station*

* the kinetoscope, the first machine to produce *motion pictures*

* and by synchronizing his phonograph and kinetoscope, he made the first *talking movies*.

With more patents than anyone before or since, Edison received a Congressional Gold Medal for developing inventions that "revolutionized civilization in the last century."

Edison Was One Bright Bulb

Your world would be very different if that one inventive genius hadn't had a hot desire for the good life. Because of the work of one person trying to make life more enjoyable, you have lights, power, music, and movies.

Not bad.

In fact, take away Thomas Edison and a couple of

other bright people—Alexander Bell and Henry Ford—and you would have no phones, no lights, no motor cars—not a single luxury. Life would be as primitive as can be.

You should be glad for those geniuses. Or maybe not.

"But that was then," you might be thinking. "This is now." Thomas Edison may have been overjoyed with a light bulb and a scratchy record player, but your dreams of the good life are bigger and better. Maybe you want several hot wheels—and not the two-inch plastic kind. A house—one with a four-story wall of glass. Money to jet around the globe—preferably in your own plane—and to own several homes away from home. A collection of toys—Jet Skis, ATVs, snowmobiles, sports equipment—a private cook and a personal trainer and a professional shopping assistant so you can possess a perfect body outfitted in perfect clothes. Don't forget your house wired full of every electronic gadget available. Oh, and don't forget—a yacht. And a maid and a butler and a chauffeur and a gardener and . . .

Getting the Good Stuff

We all have our appetites whetted by the same advertising machine. It isn't hard to dream up what the good life is supposed to look like.

I have no doubt that you want to love and be loved,

have deep friends, and avoid wasting even one second of your life in a boring job. You likely also want some version of the good life. All work and no play, after all, doesn't just make you dull. It also makes you tired. God made you to need *rest*. Even God took a break after He made the world (Genesis 2:2).

You may never be able to afford all the luxuries we just described. You might even feel unspiritual about wanting or having that much. On the other hand, you might be hoping to acquire lots of material things and figure God's will doesn't enter into it.

But you might not know that the Bible has more to say about money and things of this world than just about any other single topic. Read this straight talk about things:

* *Good things come from God*. God made it, so He owns it: "The earth is the Lord's, and everything in it, the world, and all who live in it" (Psalm 24:1). Every good thing you have is from God (James 1:17), who promises to meet "all your needs" (Philippians 4:19). And it is "the blessing of the Lord" that brings wealth (Proverbs 10:22).

* *Good things are good*. God "richly provides us with everything for our enjoyment" (1 Timothy 6:17). If God didn't want us to enjoy life, He would have made an ugly, boring world. As it

is, He put us in a beautiful, exciting place. And in God's world, money can do good things. It can buy rest, recreation, freedom, privacy, mobility, even health. It pays the church heating bill. It jets a missionary family to the other side of the world.

* *Good things break.* The fact is, having things comes with a warning: "Command those who are rich in this present world not to be arrogant nor to put their hope in wealth, *which is so uncertain*, but to put their hope in God" (1 Timothy 6:17, italics added). Note that you can't take anything with you when you die (Psalm 49:16–17).

* *Good things can get in the way of following God.* When what you have looms larger than your Lord, then you have lost sight of the limits of luxury. "No one can serve two masters," Jesus said. "Either he will hate the one and love the other, or he will be devoted to the one and despise the other. You cannot serve both God and Money" (Matthew 6:24). God may bless us with good things. But we can get life's priorities all turned around when we put things ahead of serving God and others.

Things can get in the way of understanding God's

truth for us and what He wants for our lives. Jesus said, for example, that when some people hear His truth, the truth is "choked by life's worries, riches and pleasures" (Luke 8:14).

Even though things are gifts from your Master, they can also master you. Yet this much is clear: If you want to fulfill the desire of your heart, you need to fulfill those desires God's way. That doesn't just go for love, friends, and career. It goes for getting the good things in life.

So how do we get the good things according to God's way?

A Fistful of Quarters

For Seth, every visit to his grandparents was a chance at the change jar. It was a jug with a neck just the right size for Seth to stick in one hand and pull out a fistful of quarters. Then he was off to the store for an enjoyable visit to the toy aisle.

Seth's grandparents could have turned the jar upside down and shaken out all the change. They could have smashed the jar and let their favorite grandson make off with all the money. But his grandparents knew that the amount Seth could get in just one hand was the right amount for a great time at the store.

When you delight in God, you can be satisfied with the right amount of material things. In Matthew 6:33, Jesus said, "But seek first his kingdom and his righteousness, and all these things will be given to you as well." Put God and His ways first in your life, then trust that God will take care of the rest. That is God's universal, made-for-everyone will.

You have to look back a few verses to see exactly what "all these things" are. Jesus was discussing food and drink and clothing. "Why do you worry about clothes?" He asked. "See how the lilies of the field grow. They do not labor or spin. Yet I tell you that not even Solomon in all his splendor was dressed like one of these" (Matthew 6:28–29).

If God's care for the flowers is that sure, Jesus was saying, then God's care for you is even better. People who don't know God, though, worry endlessly about things. "For the pagans run after all these things," Jesus said, "and your heavenly Father knows that you need them" (Matthew 6:32).

God's provision doesn't sound like guaranteed riches, but it doesn't sound like He wants you to starve either. It seems that Jesus is not as concerned about *what you have* as He is about *how you get it* and *what you do with it.*

How You Get What You've Got

You no doubt know we are not to steal (Exodus 20:15), whether that is shoplifting clothes, pirating software, ripping copyrighted CD or MP3 tracks, swiping test answers, or swapping homework. That is *not* part of God's plan for us to get things. Check out what God does have planned:

✴ *God is very concerned about how we get things.* The Bible is specific, for example, on how businesspeople should behave, giving principles that apply to how we barter and bargain with people. It condemns scrimping and cheating (Amos 8:5), oppressing the poor (Proverbs 22:16), wanting what your neighbor has (Exodus 20:17), and charging too much interest (Proverbs 28:8).

✴ *God is very concerned that we remember where we got our things.* That doesn't mean that you should save your receipts to show where you bought everything. It means God is the source of every good thing we have. God makes some of us with gifts that allows us to earn bushels of money. He has made a world full of good things, so it can't be wrong to aim to enjoy those things. The problem comes when we dedicate our lives to the great things God has made—rather than to our ultimate Creator (Romans 1:25). Listen to this: Scripture mocks people who melt gold and silver to make little statues to pray to (Isaiah 40:19–20). We might not mold metal into an idol, but we might have a hobby or a car or a rack of clothes that gets more of our attention than God does.

* *God is very concerned with what we do with our things.* Remember the passage from 1 Timothy 6 about God making everything for our enjoyment—and not being arrogant about money? It is followed by another insight into God's universal will: God wants you to be generous with what you have. First Timothy 6:18 says, "Command them [those who are rich] to do good, to be rich in good deeds, and to be generous and willing to share."

To be truthful, you can't predict how much wealth God will bring you. You don't know how much God will put in your hand. But from what those verses say, it looks like you need to have godly priorities; that is, keep first things first and be willing to share the wealth God gives you.

God's Big Signal

You have seen how Scripture and prayer and counsel help you to discern God's will for your life. Here's the fourth and final piece of a four-step strategy to help you understand God's best for you: interpreting your circumstances.

You have desires. Things you want. Things you don't know if you will get. And things you don't know how to obtain. That's the whole puzzle of God's will. All of your questions come down to "Does God want me to *have that?*" and "Does He want me to *go there?*" and "Should I try to *do that?*"

Reading your circumstances will tell you a lot about God's specific will for your getting things. But understanding your day-to-day circumstances is also a way of discovering God's will that applies to all of life.

Here's why. Your whole life is like Seth's change jar. You discover and uncover God's will in the real world. Your real-world *circumstances* often give you concrete feedback about what God wants. When you actually try to take hold of something, you find out what happens. Like reaching in a change jar, you pick up the quarters and when you pull out your hand you see just what you have:

* Does the college you applied to let you in—or not?

* Did you get the part-time job you applied for?

* Does the duct tape hold the transmission on your car—or do you have to do without wheels?

* Does your best friend pick up the phone when you make last-minute movie plans?

* Does she say "Yes!" when you ask her to marry you?

✳ Do your parents change their minds about your request for this or that?

✳ Do you make the grades so you can get that job and make that money and buy that house?

✳ Does your grandma get over her illness when you pray?

✳ Does God magnificently, surprisingly, freely drop what you need into your life?

Sometimes God answers a desire right away. Sometimes it takes a while. Other times He flat out says no. But here's the key: You can dream and desire all you want. You can think you have discerned God's will. But if the good things you want aren't in your hand, at some point you may have to consider it's not in God's will.

And that might be a signal from God.

Open Doors—Closed Doors

God uses circumstances to direct us.

God is sovereign—in ultimate control—over the entire universe. He can cause anything to happen in any way He wants. But often God permits things to happen that aren't what we asked for. Paul gives an example of how something he desired—and no doubt asked God to give him—didn't happen. In Romans 1:13 he wrote, "I do not want you to be unaware, brothers, that I planned many times to come to you (but have been prevented from doing so until now)." Paul is saying, "Look, I've tried to come to you. But God prevented it."

So how was God's will fulfilled in Paul's life? Through circumstances. Specifically, through a closed door. That is how Paul heard God's direction. Many times Paul planned to see his friends in Rome. Many times God directed Paul *by the way things turned out.*

Now, you have to be careful with circumstances. You always want to check the specifics of God's will for your life with prayer and counsel and knowledge of the Scriptures. Because if the going gets rough it doesn't necessarily mean the situation isn't God's will for you.

For example, let's say you are thinking about law school and you have prayed about God's will. If you apply to three schools and all three turn you down, it might be a *closed door*, a good indication from circumstances that God wants to send you into something else. However, it might be you should knock on that closed door a little bit to be sure it should stay closed. And just because a door seems wide open doesn't automatically mean you should run right through it.

Getting Through Open Doors

As you look at your life, you will see that you have both *open doors*—things that make it possible to pursue a certain desire—and *closed doors*—things that get in your way.

Open doors are your possibilities—the positive happenings in the nitty-gritty circumstances of your life. They are opportunities that you create or that come calling on their own. Here's another kind of open door you might not think about: Your biggest open doors are the variety of resources you have inside you. It's like your equipment to do good, to get God's will done. And taking stock of what equipment you have often tells you, for example, what career is best for you.

While most of us wish at some point or another we had been born in a mansion and handed life on a silver platter, those are resources *outside* of ourselves. Did you know that our real riches lie elsewhere? Our real resources are *inside* us. They are the gifts God has given each of us.

Thomas Edison had attended school for only three months when his teacher labeled him a slow learner, likely because of a hearing disorder. His family was far from wealthy, but his mother taught him to read and let him have a small laboratory in his basement. Edison knew his key resources were not his family's *means* but his God-given creative *mind*. Later in life he said, "A man is worth whatever his brain can produce."

You are suited to do all sorts of superb things. God gives all of us natural gifts. He gives us spiritual gifts. He gives us each a personality fitted to certain settings. Our gifts aren't always immediately obvious. But as you identify those inner resources from God, you may find He guides you to use them more and more. Try these questions to uncover gifts you might not realize you have:

* *Identifying your natural gifts:* What do people tell me I'm good at? What can I do well that others struggle to do? What kinds of strengths do I have in areas like organization, physical coordination, mechanical skills, an inquisitive mind, artistic or musical sense, natural people skills, or abilities to persuade and lead people?

* *Identifying your spiritual gifts:* How has God helped people through me? What causes or issues do I care deeply about? When I read the newspaper or learn about the world in school, what things would I like to see God change? Are there ministries or mission trips I've participated in at church—and what role did I play?

* *Identifying your personality:* What settings at school or work appeal to me most? Do I like to be around people—or do I need more time alone? Do I work best amid noise or quiet? Am I attracted to lots of activities or just a few? Do I see the big picture or am I good with detail?

Would I prefer to focus on people, things, or ideas?

To learn even more about how God leads you through your strengths and interests, you can read *Find Your Fit*, a whole book dedicated to helping you discover and appreciate your unique giftedness in these areas and more. It's written by human resource expert Jane Kise and my coauthor, Kevin Johnson. For more information visit Kevin's Web site, at *www.thewave.org*.

Bumping Into Closed Doors

Closed doors might not sound like much fun, but they often show us God's will. Some closed doors are negative answers to the kind of circumstantial questions we looked at above. There are also closed doors that life shuts in our faces: stressful home situations, family obligations, a lack of money, a disadvantage or disability. Other closed doors we create for ourselves: our past performance, a lazy attitude, rebellion against parents and other authority, a pregnancy or baby, a teen marriage, etc.

When those things and a million other difficulties come between us and a desire, how do we know whether to hang it up or hang in there? There are four questions to ask of ourselves and of God:

Is this closed door because of something we've done wrong?

In the Old Testament God took the kingship of Israel away from Saul and gave it to David. Why? "Because you did not obey the Lord . . . the Lord has done this to you today" (1 Samuel 28:18). Saul wanted to be king forever, but he and his sons were slain the next day.

You and I may not be a king or a queen, but we might run into a closed door because our priorities are out of balance and we are seeking things God knows aren't good for us.

We can ask God to show us something in our life that is not pleasing to Him. Like David in the Psalms asked: "Search me, O God, and know my heart; test me and know my thoughts. Point out anything in me that offends you, and lead me along the path of everlasting life" (Psalm 139:23–24 NLT).

This kind of closed door can be a big signal from God that we are out of bounds.

Is this closed door keeping us from something harmful?

"I wanted success as a musician," Monica said. "Most people wouldn't have seen it, but I was incredibly proud. My voice teachers told me I was good enough to make it professionally, but I couldn't get my attention off myself. Things just fell apart. My band went nowhere. What I see now is that God was keeping me from going somewhere that wouldn't have been good for me."

Remember the foot-stompin' three-year-olds back in

chapter 1? Sometimes we want a toy that could harm us and God is kind enough not to give it to us. He throws a hindrance in our path that stops us before we get hurt.

This kind of closed door can be a big signal from God that we are about to go off track.

Is the closed door keeping me from something I truly want?

When Tennessee Titan running back Eddie George lied to his mother about failing a high school course, she sent him hundreds of miles away to a military academy. George had left behind the starting tailback position at his home high school. After his mother told him he was going to military school, Eddie recalled, "I cried to my grandmother, I cried to anyone I could—my sister, my uncles—to stop her from making this decision. I thought my football career was over. I felt my mom was stripping me of my dreams." Instead George was forced to decide what he really wanted—to become a delinquent or to let his football skills carry him to the Super Bowl.

God sometimes sets an Eddie George kind of obstacle in our path to force us to decide what we really want. George had to choose to succeed at football even though he had been shipped to a new school, a choice that ultimately took him to the NFL. God may guide us through Scripture, prayer, and counsel, but like George we might not be applying ourselves in the proper direction. When we are confronted by a heart-stopping circumstance, we might decide we indeed do want what is on the other side of that closed door.

This kind of closed door can be a big signal from God that we should reexamine our goal.

Is the closed door something we can push through—or is it shut beyond budging?

If you are driving down a road and you find a tree has fallen across your path, you don't drive you car faster and harder into the tree. Now, if you are sure where you are headed and are determined to get there, you find a winch. You borrow a chain saw. You probably call the road department for some major help. You don't get through a roadblock without the right resources.

Wisdom on the road of life is knowing when and how to back up and muster new resources so you can plow through roadblocks. Ask yourself what good thing you want. Then ask yourself how badly you want it. And size up your obstacle to see if it is something that God could use to make you smarter and stronger.

Often what God wants to teach us is persistence and diligence. Listen to Proverbs 14:23: "All hard work brings a profit, but mere talk leads only to poverty." And Proverbs 21:5: "The plans of the diligent lead to profit as surely as haste leads to poverty." God isn't talking just about getting the goods. Hard work is necessary to achieving any goal.

This kind of closed door can be a big signal from

God that He wants to teach us persistence as we push through.

Big Wisdom About Good Things

We all want the good things God has for us. Moving along the path to obtaining what we desire, we encounter obstacles and opportunities, closed doors and open doors. Here's the final word on living the good life: Good things are good, but they aren't necessarily the best things. God's will is that you "seek first his kingdom and his righteousness." Only then will all these things "be given to you as well."

It's a fact that God put you in a beautiful world for your enjoyment. It's also a fact that He put you in a world where you can use all the resources He gives you to do good. Yet the most important truth of life is that knowing God is the most valuable goal you can have in life. Good as they may be, things ultimately won't satisfy your heart. What your heart really longs for is God, and He is what you really need. Hebrews 13:5 puts it like this: "Keep your lives free from the love of money and be content with what you have, because God has said, 'Never will I leave you; never will I forsake you.' "

CHAPTER 7

I Want to Be Close to God

There was this guy I liked," Kelli explains. "He knew I liked him, and he invited me to a Bible study with his youth group. I told him I already went to church, but then I sort of said, 'well, whatever,' and went. The first time I went I thought his church was weird. I liked the music, but it was all about God and I had never heard songs like that. People my age got into the singing. A few were crying. Lots were closing their eyes when they sang, like they were praying. Everybody seemed totally interested in God.

"Afterward this guy who invited me said I needed to know Jesus," Kelli continues. "I didn't like that. I figured my life was good. Then a couple of my friends really messed up. One got pregnant, and another got kicked out of school. That made me think about my own life. After a while I started to think that maybe there was more to God than I thought. And that maybe God did have something to do with filling the emptiness I felt inside. That's when I decided to live my whole life for

God. I'm still in shock. All I was looking for was a boy-friend. Instead I found how much I could know God now. I wouldn't trade my relationship with Him for anything."

All the Donuts in the World

I once heard about a Christian music group that never got beyond playing outreaches in church base-ments and parking lots. Their music couldn't draw a crowd, so to bait listeners closer they set a tray of do-nuts dead center in front of the stage. When people went for the donuts, the band shared their faith, inspir-ing this band motto: "They came for the donuts, but they stayed for God."

God is bigger and better than donuts. God has an-swers to all the desires of your heart, from friendship to extreme excitement to true love and meaningful work and the good things He has made for your enjoy-ment. He knows how to meet those needs because He designed you to belong, get rest, feel love, and find pur-pose and significance. God is the source of every gift— those good things you experience as you say yes to His will.

But God has something more to give you than all that.

See, God doesn't just want to give you *the world*.

He wants to give you *himself*.

God doesn't just want you to delight in *His gifts*.
He wants you to delight in *Him*.

The God-Shaped Vacuum

God made you and me to have a deep relationship with Him. God desires that we experience closeness to Him, a radically loving relationship with the God of the universe. And you know what? We can search for all the *good* things of life yet miss the *best* thing in the world.

That's what Kelli figured out. She had her eyes aimed at a great guy. But God had something for her much better than a boyfriend.

A lot of people who have everything finally come to realize that there is more to life than even those wonders. Many of them reach the same conclusion as Solomon, a man who actually devoted himself to testing all the good things of life. When he concluded his "experiments" in work, power, love, and pleasure, he surveyed everything he owned and everything he had experienced. His reaction wasn't exactly wild happiness and overwhelming contentment. In fact, listen to how Solomon spoke of his accomplishments: "Utterly meaningless! Everything is meaningless," he said (Ecclesiastes 1:2). And he added this: "When I surveyed all that my hands had done and what I had toiled to achieve, everything was meaningless, a chasing after the wind" (Ecclesiastes 2:11). Solomon ached with the emptiness that gnaws inside when God is anything but number one.

We can try to fill up our lives—even fill it up with good things—and yet never be full. Like Solomon, we feel what one person called "the God-shaped vacuum" within us. And if that emptiness is not filled with God, we will continue to live life in an endless search to satisfy our needs without ever reaching full satisfaction.

But when we put God in His rightful place in our lives, our hearts' desires make life sweet. Yet if we misplace God, those desires are like sugar packets poured straight into our gaping mouths. What God designed as complete fulfillment in our lives becomes a sweet taste that lasts only a few seconds.

Unearthing the Treasure Trove

The Bible is full of passages that point out how incredibly important it is to have a deep relationship with God. Look at a few:

* Jesus said that finding God is like finding buried treasure valuable beyond imagination: "The kingdom of heaven is like treasure hidden in a field," He said. "When a man found it, he hid it again, and then in his joy went and sold all he had and bought that field" (Matthew 13:44). Did you get that? The man sold *everything* to get the treasure!

✱ The *very first* commandment of the Ten Commandments is this: "I am the Lord your God. . . . You shall have no other gods before me" (Exodus 20:2–3).

✱ In the book of Isaiah, God asks, "To whom will you compare me? Or who is my equal?" (Isaiah 40:25). God goes on to contrast His greatness with the puniness of all the people and things you might think rank higher than Him on the list of life's important things.

✱ Paul was bold. He said that the things he thought counted in life were lower than low: "What is more, I consider everything a loss compared to the surpassing greatness of knowing Christ Jesus my Lord, for whose sake I have lost all things. I consider them rubbish" (Philippians 3:8).

✱ Have you ever considered how you will spend your time in heaven? Well, eternity is all about knowing God. Revelation puts it like this: "And I heard a loud voice from the throne saying, 'Now the dwelling of God is with men, and he will live with them. They will be his people, and God himself will be with them and be their God' " (Revelation 21:3). Jesus said, "Now this is eternal life: that they may know you, the only true God, and Jesus Christ, whom you have sent" (John 17:3).

All the good things of life—good as they are—matter not a bit compared to a life in pursuit of knowing God. Jeremiah 9:23–24 tells us, "This is what the Lord says: 'Let not the wise man boast of his wisdom or the strong man boast of his strength or the rich man boast of his riches, but let him who boasts boast about this: that he understands and knows me, that I am the Lord, who exercises kindness, justice and righteousness on earth, for in these I delight,' declares the Lord."

The Whole Point

See, when you respond to Christ, you don't simply embrace a philosophy or buy a road map showing you how to dodge through the right and wrong decisions of life. You establish a personal relationship with your loving Creator, the One who knows you thoroughly and loves you completely. You gain the privilege of enjoying and worshiping the King of the Universe in all His bright shining glory. You are eternally identified as His child, and your personal relationship with Him sets you free to be all that you were created to be.

Tell me: How could you be happier and more fulfilled in life than coming to know and love the most important Person in your life?

That's the kind of life I want.

I bet you do too.

Back to Kelli. "I know that when I figured out what it meant to really know God," she says, "my Christian life radically changed. I wasn't just playing church or looking for what I could get out of being a believer. One of the songs I learned in my new youth group tells God exactly what my heart feels: 'The greatest thing . . . in all my life . . . is knowing you.' "

Get Close and Stick Close

If knowing God is the desire of your heart and the biggest gift God has to give you, how do you get there?

God's will is that you *get close* to Him. Once you have done that, then God's will for you is that you *stick close* to Him.

Let's look at that first step first. What do we mean by "get close to God"?

From reading *God's Will, God's Best* you already know about God's universal will. And His specific will. This next part is so big that you can call it God's *ultimate* will. God's ultimate will is that you and all people would have a relationship with Him through Jesus Christ. God "wants everyone to be saved and to understand the truth" (1 Timothy 2:4 NLT).

Exactly how important is that? Well, it's the biggest point of God's will for anyone's life. If you are reading this and haven't yet accepted God's forgiveness and the new friendship He freely provides for you through

Christ's death, then God's first and only word about His will for you is that you need to trust Christ as your Savior.

Coming close to God isn't complicated. It's a matter of saying, "God, I know that I am a sinner. I have done wrong. Please forgive me. I turn—I repent—of my wrong way and trust in Jesus, who died in my place for my sins. Thank you for your forgiveness. I place my faith in you, not in myself. Help me to live close to you by following you in everything I do."

I will be honest. Until you have done that—until you have taken that first step to get close—God doesn't have much more to say to you. While everything you have learned this far is true, it won't do you much good in your life until you take this foundational step. If you don't know Christ, then God's will for you right now is to come to Him. That's *getting close* to God through the sacrificial death of Christ.

You Can Stick Close to God

Once you *get close*, then your second step is to *stick close*. When you do God's will, you experience closeness to God. When you obey what you know to be God's will, you and God are on the same road. You are in the same spot. But if the Christian life is like a bike ride, the strength to do God's will doesn't come from swallowing hard and pedaling fast. I know too many Christians who try in their own strength to grow spiritually.

Here's what I mean. Suppose you are sure that you are a Christian but you are burned out and bored with your faith. Spiritual duties like prayer and Bible study and telling others about God are things you do and do—but mostly to prove yourself to God and earn His acceptance.

But here's what you might be missing: When you belong to God He already sees you as His eternally lovable, infinitely valuable, and thoroughly competent daughter or son. Nothing you do on your own attracts God's attention or wins His care for you. Your status as God's child and all the blessings that come with it stem from what He has made you and what He has done for you because of Christ.

Think about it. If you serve a God who thinks you are lovable, valuable, and competent, doesn't that change your perspective of prayer or study or any form of obedience? You stop moaning, "I've got to!" and start thinking, "I get to!"

You can wake up and say, "God, I know you are on my side because I am your child. You accept me and love me and I'm going to live in a way that says thanks for that. I know you have an exciting day planned for me today." That sure beats thinking, "God, you're out to get me." Or, "God, you've disliked me from the day you first saw me and you don't care for me." Or, "God, I'm going to spend my whole day trying to convince you to love me." The difference between those two mind-sets is the difference between living in God's kingly palace as an heir or as a slave.

I remember that about a year after I became a Christian I came to a conscious choice that I not only wanted to *get* close to God, I wanted to *stick* close to Him too. I didn't just want Christ as my Savior, I was going to follow Him as my Lord. I came to the point where I said, "God, here's my life, my future, with all my limitations, everything. And I submit my entire life to you. Take my life and do with it what you want." That was when I stopped groaning and started growing.

The Growing Edge

Once you understand that you are God's precious child, it is true that He has things for you to do. But what you do starts with who you are. When you really know you are God's forgiven friend, you can start acting like it. Sticking close to God doesn't happen by making yourself *act* holy. It happens because you already *are* holy in His sight.

That's the kind of knowledge that puts you on the growing edge of God's will. Did you know that your bones, for example, don't grow all over? Like those long bones in your legs that just keep getting longer, so that again and again your parents have to take you shopping for pants—they don't grow throughout the bone. They grow at special points called "growth plates." That's where the action is.

Now, spiritually, that's where we want to be. That is where we can live life on the growing edge of knowing and applying God's best for our lives. My friend David Ferguson says every believer should be able to answer the question, "What is God working on in you today?" It is an exciting thing to know what God wants to do in our lives. You see God working on this and improving that. You sense growth and maturity.

Repairing Your Relationship With God

Do you know that one of the saddest things I see is Christian young people who don't know how to get their relationship with God back on good footing when they have failed?

Rachel was seventeen when she got pregnant. She was sure God was done with her. "God could never want me back," she thought. "I've blown it forever. Everybody—even God—thinks I'm a slut. So I might as well live that way." Rachel was sure God could never accept her again or show her the right way to handle her problem. She needed to know how to get close to God again.

Remember Adam and Eve in the Garden of Eden? Handmade by God for each other, totally in love. They enjoyed absolute, transparent friendship with each other and with God. And Adam and Eve knew God's clear will: They could eat fruit from any tree in the garden *except* for the "tree of the knowledge of good and evil."

"Hmm . . ." they thought. "We think we would be happier if we could eat the forbidden fruit." You know the rest. They ate. They broke God's command. They took it upon themselves to decide what was best instead of believing God knew what was best.

In a million ways—some big, some small—we all are just like that. Sin happens when you choose something other than what God has chosen for you. When you think something else can make you deliriously happy instead of what He has for you. When you make anything other than God number one in your life.

Jesus' disciple John wrote that eternal life is all about knowing God. Later in his life, John said this: "My dear children, I am writing this to you so that you will not sin. But if you do sin, there is someone to plead for you before the Father. He is Jesus Christ, the one who pleases God completely. He is the sacrifice for our sins. He takes away not only our sins but the sins of all the world" (1 John 2:1–2 NLT).

See, God knows that none of us does His will perfectly. Sometimes we don't choose God's best. We sin. We get off God's path. But God has given us a way to get back on track. God doesn't want us to sin, because sin still unravels our lives. It hurts God, each of us, and often the people around us. But when we sin, here is God's clear promise: "If we confess our sins to him, he is faithful and just to forgive us and to cleanse us from every wrong" (1 John 1:9 NLT).

Rachel was able to take hold of God's forgiveness and got close again with God, and her life changed. She still had to deal with the consequences of being a young, unmarried mom. But she did it with the strength God gives. She got back on track.

This One's for You—and for the Whole World

Did you know that your life is filled with people who aren't close to God? It's great to know that Christ is your Savior and Lord. But God doesn't intend for you to keep that good situation to yourself. This is one point of God's universal will I haven't said much about so far. But remember? God "wants *everyone* to be saved and to understand the truth" (1 Timothy 2:4 NLT, italics added). That includes you. It also extends to the whole world.

As a Christian you have the privilege of inviting others to experience the closeness to God you already possess. In fact, there is a no-doubt-about-it command that tells us to share our faith. It's in Matthew 28:19–20, a passage students of the Bible call the Great Commission. Here's what it says: "Therefore, go and make disciples of all the nations, baptizing them in the name of the Father and the Son and the Holy Spirit. Teach these new disciples to obey all the commands I have given you" (NLT).

Just because your church hangs up a banner bearing that verse when missionaries come to town doesn't mean it's only for full-time workers in foreign countries. The will of God for all believers is to share their faith. "But, God," you might be wondering, "should I share with my friends at school?" Why, the Bible says to go into all the world and spread the Good News. Doesn't that include everywhere? Doesn't that encompass our friends? We don't have to pray about it. God has already revealed His clear will.

Early in my Christian life I found that in this area of obeying God I was concerned about everybody everywhere in the world—except for the people right around me. I prayed for people in the Congo. And China. Why? I didn't have to get involved with them. As soon as I started to pray for my neighbor, my friend, the person I sat next to, the person behind me, then all of a sudden a little voice inside me said, "Look, why don't you talk to him?"

I still find this true of high school students. They get together at the pole or before school and pray for everyone on campus except for the kid who has sat next to them in homeroom for the past two years. They pray for their third cousin in Toledo and for the spread of God's Good News in Sudan. That's good. But why leave out your next-desk neighbor?

The fact that it's God's will for us to share our faith doesn't mean we shouldn't seek His will about *how* or *where* we could spread God's Good News best. In high school, sharing your faith may not look like what you expect. You can get involved in team sports and group activities like drama or choir or band or the school newspaper. It's in those settings that you figure out how to share with other people. You discover what works and what doesn't as you tell others about Christ. Each of us need to be as Peter said, "You must worship Christ as Lord of your life. And if you are asked about your Christian hope, always be ready to explain it" (1 Peter 3:15 NLT).

Just Say, "I Do."

A few nights ago on TV there was a show about weird things that happen at weddings. Grooms got sick. Brides got stung by bees. Huge wedding cakes tumbled through the air, and church floors flooded. But the worst was the groom run off the road in a car accident. In great pain the husband-to-be struggled through the ceremony, then he spent the next three weeks in the hospital—due to the car accident, in case you were wondering, not the ceremony.

You know what? No groom, no honeymoon.

Becoming a Christian without living your faith every moment of every day is, well, absurd. It's ludicrous. It's like getting married and not accompanying your spouse on the honeymoon. Love isn't supposed to happen like that. You are designed to enjoy your identity as a newlywed. Faith isn't supposed to happen like that. You are designed to enjoy your identity as God's child.

It's only when you stick close to God that you fully enjoy all the privileges of being a believer. You get to stay close to God—to borrow some words you might have heard before—for better and for worse, for richer or for poorer, in sickness and in health. Ponder the deep closeness to God in this verse: "Better is one day in your courts than a thousand elsewhere; I would rather be a doorkeeper in the house of my God than dwell in the tents of the wicked" (Psalm 84:10). And in this one: "You have made known to me the path of life; you will fill me with joy in your presence" (Psalm 16:11).

God alone is the one who can fulfill the deepest desires of your heart.

Do you want that?

Then say "I do" to God.

And live like you mean it.

CHAPTER 8

I Want My Life to Matter

Tanya's classmates wiped their tears as they walked slowly down the center church aisle, filing out past Tanya's casket. Friend after friend had stood at a microphone and told how Tanya had impacted their lives. Tanya's youth pastor had recounted how her enthusiastic involvement in an after-school program for latchkey children had brought other helpers into the program and spared dozens of kids from troubled loneliness. Tanya was the heart and soul of that ministry, and with her life instantly cut short by a rare heart condition, she left a huge void. Her friends wondered how anyone so young could have accomplished so much.

What Will You Be Remembered For?

Picture a crowd of your friends and family milling around in a church lobby. Post-funeral. Post-*your*-funeral, that is. They chitchat. They sip coffee. They nibble cake. Now, what do you hope is going on? For starters, you would feel incredibly sad if people didn't cry because they missed you. You want tears—here a *sob*, there a *sob*, better yet, everywhere a *sob sob*. And besides that, you would want them to say exceedingly kind things about you. You hope they mutter something deeper than "Easy come, easy go!" or "Good riddance!" or "Can I have his bedroom?"

You would hope people thought your life mattered. You would want them to say the world is a better place because you were here. You would want them to be certain you spent your life doing the right things.

But what could make your life matter? What would make it *significant*?

Every third grader who ever broke a school record for doing more sit-ups than anyone else wanted his or her achievement to stand forever. Intellectuals and politicians and generals dream that their contributions will be remembered in textbooks and statues and monuments.

So what will it be for you? Maybe at school or church you have written your own epitaph, the words carved on a gravestone to capture the meaning of a life. Think of all the ways people big and small strive to be remembered and then try to sum up your life. Take your pick of what you want chiseled on your memorial:

* *"I made millions."* Jesus pointed out that money doesn't count for eternity. He said this of the man who had done nothing in life but

make money: "You fool! This very night your
life will be demanded from you. Then who will
get what you have prepared for yourself?"
(Luke 12:20). Jesus said the end would be pit-
iful for anyone who "stores up things for himself but is not rich toward God" (Luke 12:21).

* *"I was incredibly famous."* Fame and power
wear out even faster than money: "He [God]
brings princes to naught and reduces the rul-
ers of this world to nothing. No sooner are they
planted, no sooner are they sown, no sooner do
they take root in the ground, than he blows on
them and they wither, and a whirlwind sweeps
them away like chaff" (Isaiah 40:23–24).

* *"I loved my family and friends."* Now we're getting warmer. God made loving people second in
importance only to loving Him, so we know
that loving others is a worthwhile accomplish-
ment. Former U.S. President George Bush
summed it up well in an interview with the
folks at *www.achievement.org*: "Politics is important, sitting at the head table is glamorous.
Traveling around the world, trying to do something for world peace was wonderful. But family and friends and faith are what really matters in life. . . . The proudest thing in my life is
that my children come home."

✳ *"I lived for God."* Here's the one way I think any of us can live a life that truly matters. It's the whole reason Jesus came and died: "And he [Jesus] died for all, that those who live should no longer live for themselves but for him who died for them and was raised again" (2 Corinthians 5:15). If God invested the life of His Son to enable us to live for Him, then living for God and others must matter.

Living for God is the only way to have a true sense of significance. Living for God brings life meaning beyond imagination. There is perhaps no greater feeling than God working through your life to accomplish His purpose. To sense God involving you in His ministry to another person is an experience like no other.

God's Significant Plan for You

We need to make one point clear. As exciting as it is to *do* significant things, we already *are* eternally significant. As a beloved child of God, you have an importance that will never be matched by anything you ever do. If you were the only person ever created, Jesus would have died for you just to form a relationship with you. Remember from last chapter? When you belong to God, you are eternally lovable, infinitely valuable, and thoroughly competent. You can't do a single thing to boost your status as God's child.

But chances are that you want to *do* something significant in this life. You want to make a difference, to leave the world better than you found it.

God wants that brand of significance for you too. After all, you are his "masterpiece," designed by Him to do good works (Ephesians 2:10 NLT). Paul had a commitment to do God's plan. In Acts 20:24 he wrote, "I consider my life worth nothing to me, if only I may finish the race and complete the task the Lord Jesus has given me—the task of testifying to the gospel of God's grace." Paul dedicated his whole life to the specific task God gave him. In other words, he found significance in *doing God's will.*

See, the most significant life you could ever lead grows out of your knowing God's will and following His plan. You fulfill your desire for significance when you apply the things you have learned in *God's Will, God's Best*—and all the things God teaches you from here forward.

Jesus, our example, said, "My food . . . is to do the will of him who sent me and to finish his work" (John 4:34).

Paul, too, backed up his strong desire with actions. In God's strength, through triumphs and suffering and hard work, he accomplished what God planned for him to do. Late in life Paul was able to say, "The time has come for my departure. I have fought the good fight, I have finished the race, I have kept the faith" (2 Timothy 4:6–7).

That's significance—finishing what God gives you to do, doing His will to the end!

As a Christian actively looking for God's guidance, you can be sure that whatever plan God has for you will make your life matter more than you can ever imagine.

Doing Your Delight

Knowing and living God's will is a lot harder than reading about it.

We can learn and understand God's universal will. We can even discover God's specific will for each area of our lives. But we still may not see God's will for a specific decision in life. Sometimes we might feel confused. Sometimes things may not be clear. But God is there to help you find His will and give you the desires of your heart.

Remember our verse from the beginning? Psalm 37: 4 says, "Delight yourself in the Lord and he will give you the desires of your heart." When God is the first thing in your life, it's a promise: He will give you the desires of your heart. That means when your life belongs to God and you are following His will, He wants you to live out your godly desires. Let me remind you again how that is biblical.

First, *it is God who guides you.* God inspired David to write this absolutely trustworthy Scripture passage. You likely know the first part, but you might never have thought about the end: "The Lord is my shepherd, I shall not be in want. He makes me lie down in green pastures, he leads me beside quiet waters, he restores my soul. *He guides me in paths of righteousness for his name's sake"* (Psalm 23:1–3, italics added). Catch that last part? You can trust that if your desire isn't God's will, He will show you. Why? When you belong to Him, nothing less than the honor and glory of God's good name guarantees that He will guide you. It's your job to listen, to be receptive, to obey. It's His job to show you.

Second, when your life conforms to God's universal will and you have sought His specific will, *He promises to shape your desires.* Remember the promise of Romans 12:1–2? When you submit to God and are transformed by the renewing of your mind, "Then you will be able to test and approve what God's will is—his good, pleasing and perfect will." God's thoughts get into your thoughts. His desires become your desires.

But even when we seek and sense God's will through Scripture, prayer, counsel, and circumstances, it doesn't mean God is going to let you see into your future.

Walking One Step at a Time

If you are like a lot of students, you might want to know *all* of God's specific will *right now.* But God usually leads you one step at a time. You might be wondering, "God, what's your will for me for the next ten years?" A ninth grader may come up to me who wants to know in detail what college he or she should attend and what major they should pick. Or a college freshman may want to know what job God plans for him or her and where to live after graduation. God is interested in that person's future—and yours. But He is more interested in obedience today—like doing your homework so you know what you are good at and what you like so *then* He can show you what to do after graduation. Like Jesus said, "Therefore do not worry about tomorrow, for tomorrow will worry about itself. Each day has enough trouble of its own" (Matthew 6:34).

God often shows us in amazing detail what to do right now. But when it comes to showing us our future, He usually leaves things a little hazy. God doesn't often give us the details and the foresight of such things as whom we will marry, where we will live, how many kids we will have, or what career we will follow. God wants to reveal His will to us, but He wants us to trust our future with Him.

The Bible, in fact, warns people who want to take too much control of their future. James 4:13–16 says: "Now listen, you who say, 'Today or tomorrow we will go to this or that city, spend a year there, carry on business and make money.' Why, you do not even know what will happen tomorrow. What is your life? You are a mist that appears for a little while and then vanishes. Instead, you ought to say, 'If it is the Lord's will, we will live and do this or that.' As it is, you boast and brag. All such boasting is evil." True vision from God always comes mixed with a healthy dose of humility toward your ability to peer very far into the future—and a whole lot of a minute-by-minute dependence on God.

God guides you one step at a time for two simple reasons.

If He told you more, you probably couldn't handle it.

If He told you more, you might not think you needed him.

Imagine if John Kennedy had known as a ten-year-old—or a seventeen-year-old—what his life would hold. He couldn't begin to understand or grapple with piloting a boat in World War II . . . sinking in the South Pacific . . . becoming the youngest person ever elected President of the United States . . . being assassinated. Can you imagine knowing those events ahead of time? It would be too much for any of us.

So God's kind understanding of your human limitations is one reason He doesn't tell us everything today. Then there's the other reason: You might think you don't need Him.

Earlier in the book I said that finding God's will isn't like unearthing a buried treasure that lets you retire on easy street and never work again. God leads you little by little in order to keep you close to Him.

"Josh," you might be thinking, "isn't that like being on a leash?" No. It's what it means to be in love with God. He counts on you to walk step by step in relationship with Him and learn from Him—getting close and staying close, because after all, finding your heart's desire is all about delighting in Him.

I don't know much of my future. I have some ideas. I have some desires and dreams. I can think of things that would be fun to see happen in my family, my ministry, and my personal life. But I know one thing. I know God's will for me today. I know God's will for me tomorrow. And I am just taking one step at a time.

Don't get impatient. You have to live with the truth that you don't and you won't know things too far in advance. What you don't need to know, God won't tell you. What you do, He will. And if you come to a point where you *must* make a decision and God seems quiet? Then He is probably saying, "You pick!"

Take a Deep Breath

As you finish this book and continue to strive to make following God's will a real, daily practice of your life, you will need three indispensable attitudes:

✳ *Indispensable Attitude #1: I am going to stay submitted.* Like I said a minute ago, guidance is God's responsibility. Listening is yours. You can be sure your ears are unplugged to hear and do God's will by daily submitting your life to God, telling Him you want what He wants. Psalm 139:23–24 provides great words to pray if you are short on inspiration: "Search me, O God, and know my heart; test me and know my anxious thoughts. See if there is any offensive way in me, and lead me in the way everlasting."

✴ *Indispensable Attitude #2: I am going to obey today.* James 1:22 says, "Do not merely listen to the word, and so deceive yourselves. Do what it says." Make every effort to obey quickly everything as you discover God's will, first through Scripture, then through prayer, counsel, and circumstances.

✴ *Indispensable Attitude #3: I am going to dream big.* God wants to direct you. But that doesn't take away your need to dream. Think about how God could grow you. How He could love through you. How He might use you if you were a teacher . . . a doctor . . . a construction worker . . . a stay-at-home parent . . . a musician . . . a politician. You have a choice in how you use your freedom. Paul puts it this way: "You, my brothers, were called to be free. But do not use your freedom to indulge the sinful nature; rather, serve one another in love" (Galatians 5:13). Dream big of all the ways God could be glorified through you.

When you have those attitudes, I guarantee you can't fail in finding God's best and fulfilling—in God's way and God's time—the deepest desires of your heart!

Books by Josh McDowell

BOOKS FOR YOUTH

Don't Check Your Brains at the Door
God's Will, God's Best[1]
The Teenage Q & A Book
The Truth Slayers
The Love Killers
Under Siege
Project 911 Collection
(8 small books on youth crisis issues)
Friendship 911 Workbook
Setting You Free to Make Right Choices Workbook

BOOKS FOR ADULTS

The Disconnected Generation
Right From Wrong
The New Tolerance
Handbook on Counseling Youth
The Truth Matters Workbook

For more information on Josh McDowell product,
visit your local Christian bookstore or visit www.josh.org

[1]with Kevin Johnson

Books By Kevin Johnson

Pray the Scriptures Bible
Pray the Scriptures
Pray the Scriptures When Life Hurts
KJV Pray the Scriptures Bible

EARLY TEEN DEVOTIONALS

Can I Be a Christian Without Being Weird?
Could Someone Wake Me Up Before I Drool on the Desk?
Does Anybody Know What Planet My Parents Are From?
So Who Says I Have to Act My Age?
Was That a Balloon or Did Your Head Just Pop?
Who Should I Listen To?
Why Can't My Life Be a Summer Vacation?
Why Is God Looking for Friends?
Total Devotion

EARLY TEEN DISCIPLESHIP

Get God: Make Friends With the King of the Universe
Wise Up: Stand Clear of the Unsmartness of Sin

BOOKS FOR YOUTH

Catch the Wave!
Find Your Fit[1]
Find Your Fit Discovery Workbook[1]
God's Will, God's Best[2]
Jesus Among Other Gods: Youth Edition[3]
Look Who's Toast Now!
What Do Ya Know?
What's With the Dudes at the Door?[4]
What's With the Mutant in the Microscope?[4]

To find out more about Kevin Johnson's books,
visit his website: www.kevinjohnsonbooks.com

[1]with Jane Kise   [2]with Josh McDowell   [3]with Ravi Zacharias   [4]with James White